Leading the Assembly in Prayer

A Practical Guide for Lay and Ordained Presiders

Michael J. Begolly

Resource Publications, Inc.
San Jose, California

Reprint Department
Resource Publications, Inc.
160 E. Virginia Street #290
San Jose, CA 95112-5876
1-408-286-8505 (voice)
1-408-287-8748 (fax)

Library of Congress Cataloging in Publication Data
Begolly, Michael J., 1953-
   Leading the assembly in prayer : a practical guide for lay and ordained presiders / Michael J. Begolly.
      p.   cm.
   Includes bibliographical references.
   ISBN 0-89390-398-1 (pbk.)
      1. Public worship—Catholic Church. 2. Catholic Church—Liturgy.
   3. Prayer—Catholic Church. I. Title.
   BX1970.B415   1997
   264'.02—dc21   97-5326

Printed in the United States of America

01 00 99 98 97 | 5 4 3 2 1

Editorial director: Nick Wagner
Prepress manager: Elizabeth J. Asborno
Copyeditor: Sharron S. Wood
Production assistants: Mike Sagara, David Dunlap

For my parents,
Mary Lou and Syl,
who taught me how to pray

Contents

PART TWO: Presiding at Specific Liturgical Celebrations

Acknowledgments

This book grew out of my doctoral studies at The Catholic Theological Union at Chicago, where I began to explore the intimate relationship between the presider and the liturgical assembly under the direction of my mentor and friend, Edward Foley, Capuchin. I extend my gratitude to Ed for his inspiration, encouragement, and faithful support throughout my studies and throughout the writing of this book.

I would also like to thank a dear friend and colleague, Claudia Muro, for her critical insights and thoughtful recommendations with regard to the content of the book and for her constant encouragement throughout my studies.

Several other colleagues in ministry assisted in the editing process, and to them I owe a debt of gratitude: Arlene McGannon, Susan Jenny, SC, and Mary Pellegrino, CSJ. In a special way, Mary's background in journalism proved a valuable resource in the final editing process. Her sense of humor helped me to keep the project in perspective.

Many others have helped to teach me how to preside with a sensitivity to the liturgical assembly. I am particularly grateful to the members of the communities where I have been privileged to preside at liturgy: St. Thomas More University Parish, Indiana, Pennsylvania; Seton Hill College, Greensburg, Pennsylvania; St. Francis of Assisi Parish, Orland Park, Illinois; Mother of Sorrows Parish, Murrysville, Pennsylvania; SS. Simon and Jude Parish, Blairsville, Pennsylvania; and St. Paul Parish, Greensburg, Pennsylvania.

Finally, I would like to thank my family and friends who have encouraged me by their support and have led me deeper into prayer by their faithfulness.

Acknowledgments

Acknowledgment is extended to the copyright holders who granted permission to reprint the following:

Excerpts reprinted from "The Presider" by Gabe Huck. *Liturgy with Style and Grace*, © 1984. Archdiocese of Chicago: Liturgy Training Publications. 1800 N. Hermitage Ave., Chicago, IL 60622-1101. 1-800-933-1800. All rights reserved. Used with permission.

Excerpts reprinted from *Method in Ministry: Theological Reflection and Christian Ministry* by James D. Whitehead and Evelyn Eaton Whitehead, © 1995 Whitehead Associates. Used with permission.

Excerpts from *Environment and Art in Catholic Worship* © 1978 United States Catholic Conference (USCC), Washington, DC 20017; *Music in Catholic Worship* © 1983 USCC; *Fulfilled in Your Hearing* © 1982 USCC; and *Sunday Celebrations in the Absence of a Priest: Leader's Edition* © 1994 USCC are used with permission.

Excerpts from *Strong, Loving and Wise* by Robert Hovda © 1976 The Liturgical Press (TLP); *Principles of the Liturgy* edited by Aimé-Georges Martimort © 1987 TLP; *Elements of Rite* by Aidan Kavanagh © 1982 TLP; *Mystagogy* by Enrico Mazza © 1989 Pueblo Publishing Co. Used with permission.

Excerpts from *Touchstones in Liturgical Ministry* edited by Virginia Sloyan © 1978 The Liturgical Conference. Used with permission.

The English translation of the Constitution on the Sacred Liturgy, Directory for Masses with Children, and the General Instruction of the Roman Missal from *Documents on the Liturgy, 1963-1979: Conciliar, Papal, and Curial Texts* © 1982, International Commission on English in the Liturgy, Inc. All rights reserved.

Excerpts reprinted from *Ritual and Pastoral Care* by Elaine Ramshaw, copyright © 1987 Augsburg Publishing House; and from *The Prophetic Imagination* by Walter Brueggemann, copyright © 1978 Fortress Press. Used by permission of Augsburg Fortress.

Excerpts from *Leading the Prayer of God's People* by Association of National Secretaries of Europe © 1991 Columba Press; *Gather Around the Lord* by Sean Swayne © 1987 Columba Press. Used with permission.

Excerpts from *The Promise of Partnership: A Model for Collaborative Ministry* by James D. Whitehead and Evelyn Eaton Whitehead, © 1993 HarperCollins Publishers; and from *Sharing Faith: A Comprehensive Approach to Religious Education and Pastoral Ministry* by Thomas H. Groome, © 1991 by Thomas H. Groome. Reprinted by permission of HarperCollins Publishers, Inc.

In the event that some source or copyright holder has been overlooked, please send acknowledgment requirements to the editorial director at Resource Publications, Inc.

Introduction

Debra is a pastoral associate in a large suburban parish. Recently, the pastor asked her if she would be willing to lead a wake service at the funeral home on the evening before a parishioner's funeral. After reading through the "Vigil for the Deceased" in the *Order of Christian Funerals*, she felt confident that she could lead the service. The next evening, she went to the funeral home and conducted the wake service. Debra did everything right, following the prayers in the book word for word. But afterward, she felt that something was wrong. She went back to the pastor and asked, "Is there more to leading prayer than just following the words in the book?"

Marcos is the coordinator of religious education in a small rural parish. After learning how to lead the celebration of Liturgy of the Word with children, he organized a team of eight volunteers to lead Liturgy of the Word with children at both weekend Masses in the parish. Some of the volunteers are older, some younger; some more traditional in the way they view the church, some more progressive. Many have their own ideas about how the service should be conducted. Marcos wonders how to help the volunteers see that the liturgy is bigger than their own personal interests. At the same time, he wonders how to help them integrate their personal spirituality into their ministry as leaders of public prayer.

Roberta leads a weekly communion service at St. Benedict Parish on the pastor's day off. Recently, the pastor and the parish liturgy team decided to introduce the celebration of Morning

Prayer in place of the weekly communion service. Roberta volunteered to lead Morning Prayer, but the liturgy team has another idea. They want to invite others to share in the ministry of leading prayer. Roberta doesn't understand why she can't lead Morning Prayer by herself, just as she led the communion service for the past three years. How does the liturgy team help Roberta to see that ministry is a gift to be shared? How does the team recruit and train others to be effective leaders at Morning Prayer?

Fr. Lance has been ordained for thirty-five years. He was trained to celebrate Mass in the days before Vatican II. After the Council, he quickly embraced the "new liturgy" and has kept up with all the liturgical changes. After his recent transfer to a new parish, one of the parishioners complained that the celebration of Mass was too informal with all the "chatty" comments that Fr. Lance added to the liturgy. Fr. Lance explained that he preferred a "casual" style of celebrating the liturgy so that people would feel at ease. After hearing similar complaints from several other people, Fr. Lance began to question if his way of leading prayer was, indeed, too informal. He wondered how to evaluate constructively his style of presiding.

Today, more and more people within the church are called to lead prayer. People like Debra, Marcos, Roberta, and Fr. Lance do so as officially designated ministers of the church. In preparation for this ministry, it is important for them to have proper formation in the art of leading the public prayer of the church. As they continue in this role, it is equally important that they take time to reflect on how effectively they are fulfilling their ministry.

Effective presiding involves much more than simply reading prayers from a book. It presupposes an attentiveness to God's people who have gathered to pray and a knowledge of the church's liturgical traditions. It demands a willingness to learn the basic skills of leading prayer and a commitment to grow in the exercise of this ministry. It calls for a spirit of collaboration with others in the planning and celebration of the liturgy.

Prior to the Second Vatican Council, the role of prayer leader belonged almost exclusively to the priest. The priest celebrated Mass and the sacraments according to the directions in the official books of the church. Seminarians and priests were trained to follow the rubrics of the Roman Missal, which gave strict guidelines on how to say the prayers at Mass, how to stand, and how to gesture. Numerous books were written to interpret the rubrics, and manuals were provided to newly ordained priests, which emphasized and clarified certain precepts. Little was left to the imagination, and virtually nothing was left to personal style or individualized interpretation. For example, in his *Pastoral Manual for New Priests*, Thomas Casey writes:

- "Do not turn the body at an angle when genuflecting on the first step of the altar. It is more correct and more in keeping with the importance of the altar to keep the body facing the altar at this time" (50).

- "Observe the time limits suggested in all books on the celebration of the Mass which counsel a minimum time of twenty-five minutes and a maximum time of thirty-five minutes" (51).

- "The correct position of the hands should be maintained when they are in the extended position. This means that the hands are to be held at the width and height of the shoulders and at the same level with palms facing, fingers together. To have one hand held higher than the other, to have hands out beyond the shoulders, or to have them around the level of the waist are all incorrect and serve to distract the congregation" (51).

- "On turning to the people keep the eyes down. The celebrant is not allowed to look around the church at this

time. His own concentration on the Mass and the
people's attention to the sacrifice are upset by raising the
eyes to look out into the church" (51).

Such emphasis on the correct observance of the rubrics was rooted
in the belief that the priest was acting *in persona Christi*. The priest
was seen as the mediator between God and humanity, continuing the
work of Christ the High Priest. He was the one empowered to offer
the Mass in the person of Christ for the salvation of the world. Because
the priest was entrusted with such a noble task, a great deal of emphasis
was placed on making sure the sacrifice was offered properly. This
was accomplished by strict adherence to the directives established by
the church, by neither adding to nor subtracting from the rubrics under
the penalty of, "at least, venial sin" (Zualdi xiii).

Great significance was placed upon the priest's interior disposition,
on the holiness of the sacramental action, and on the correct execution
of the rubrics. This attention to exact observance created a detached
and emotionless manner of relating to the congregation. In celebrating
the Mass, the priest was not to express his feelings or emotions. The
"faceless priest" was the ideal.[1] This ideal became a reality in the lives
of many presiders. Celebrating Mass with their backs to the people
certainly facilitated this faceless image.

In light of the reforms of Vatican II, however, this impersonal style
of presiding, once considered a virtue, is now viewed unfavorably.
Books written since Vatican II for ordained and lay presiders encourage a more prayerful and personal style of leadership at worship (see
Hovda, *Strong Loving and Wise*; Hughes, *Lay Presiding*; Kavanagh;

---

1 Godfrey Diekmann, OSB, one of the pioneers of liturgical reform in the United
States, recalls a typical exercise from a priest's retreat in pre-Vatican II days. He
describes the "dry Mass" as an experience in which "someone, usually the retreat
master, went through the motions of celebrating the Eucharist, meanwhile exhorting
his listeners to the correctness of rubrical performance. He reminded them that, since
the Mass effected its results *ex opere operato*, and above all, since Christ himself
continued to be the chief celebrant and they only represented him, they must not allow
any personal emotion or interpretation to find expression in their actions. There was to
be nothing subjective. Their ideal was to remain the faceless priest" (vii).

and Smolarski). Presiders are encouraged to manifest a committed and transparent faith, to place a high value on personal communication and respect for others, and to allow members of the assembly to exercise their proper roles of ministry. The presider is to be a person of the church, a bearer of Christian tradition, and a leader of prayer in the midst of the community.

Presiders are also encouraged now to befriend their bodies, to see the body as a sacrament of presence to the community (see Empereur). Because the liturgy is to connect with ordinary human experience and daily life, the presider is now challenged to develop a style of leadership that is more personal and attentive to the community and its life experience. Far from the pre-Vatican II ideal of obliterating the self in the liturgical celebration, the presider must bring "the whole person, the real person, the true person, the full and complete person" to this ministry (Hovda, *Strong, Loving, and Wise*, 56-7).

The Second Vatican Council, particularly in the document *Constitution on the Sacred Liturgy*, called for a greater involvement on the part of the faithful in the celebration of the liturgy (14, 26-32). As a result, the assembly is now viewed as a primary liturgical symbol, forming the context for the liturgical ministries exercised by the faithful. All members of the assembly are called to full, conscious, and active participation.

At Mass, lay persons now function as altar servers, ministers of hospitality, readers, special ministers of the Eucharist, and music ministers. At other liturgical celebrations, lay persons are empowered to preside over the assembly and lead its prayer. For example, when a priest or deacon is not available, lay persons may preside at the funeral vigil and the rite of committal (*Order of Christian Funerals* 14). During the catechumenate, the bishop may depute catechists to celebrate the exorcisms and blessings with the catechumens (*Rite of Christian Initiation of Adults* 16). Lay adults may lead celebrations of the Liturgy of the Word with children (*Directory for Masses with Children* 17). In the absence of a priest, the bishop may appoint lay persons to lead Sunday celebrations (*Sunday Celebrations in the Absence of a Priest: Leader's Edition* 21-24).

Introduction

As more and more people are called to lead liturgical celebrations, there is a corresponding obligation on the part of the church to help them learn how to preside effectively. This book is for those who are beginning this ministry as well as for those who have been presiding for some time. For beginners, it defines the ministry of the presider within the liturgical assembly and describes some basic attitudes and skills needed to preside effectively in today's church. For those with experience, it provides an opportunity to review the basic skills and to use the process of theological reflection as an impetus for refining those skills. For both, it includes a look at some practical aspects of presiding.

Document Abbreviations Used in This Book

CSL = *Constitution on the Sacred Liturgy*

DMC = *Directory for Masses with Children*

DSCAP = *Directory for Sunday Celebrations in the Absence of a Priest*

EACW = *Environment and Art in Catholic Worship*

FIYH = *Fulfilled in Your Hearing*

GIRM = *General Instruction of the Roman Missal*

LMC = *Lectionary for Masses with Children*

OCF = *Order of Christian Funerals*

MCW = *Music in Catholic Worship*

RCIA = *Rite of Christian Initiation of Adults*

SCAP = *Sunday Celebrations in the Absence of a Priest: Leader's Edition*

PART ONE

Presiding within the Liturgical Assembly

By definition, liturgy is the public prayer of the church. This implies that when the liturgy is celebrated, it is done within the community of God's people, who have come together for worship. This gathered community, the liturgical assembly, becomes the setting in which God's Word is proclaimed and the sacraments are celebrated.

It is important that those who are called to lead liturgical prayer understand the theology of the assembly as it is found in the rites and in the liturgical documents of the church. This knowledge will help the presider discover the primacy of the assembly as the context for shaping the presider's ministry.

The first part of this book situates the role of the presider within the liturgical assembly and suggests a number of skills and attitudes necessary for effective presiding.

1. The Liturgical Assembly

Mother of Sorrows Church was filled at the start of the liturgy, as it is every Sunday morning. When the procession started down the aisle, the ministers were greeted by the glorious sound of seven hundred voices in the assembly raising a song of praise to God.

As Msgr. Conway reached the sanctuary and looked out into the faces of the assembly, he smiled with delight at the community that had gathered. The parish staff, the pastoral council, and the parish as a whole had committed themselves to making the Sunday Eucharist the heart of parish life. It seemed their efforts were paying off. Ministers of hospitality, music, Word, and Eucharist helped the members of the community to celebrate their living faith. It was an inspiring experience for Msgr. Conway to preside over this assembly of God's people transformed into the Body of Christ.

One of the joys of presiding is being able to experience the power of God's Spirit at work in the people of God who gather to worship. Msgr. Conway's experience is typical where time and resources are invested in providing liturgical celebrations of good quality, where the liturgy both forms and celebrates the faith of the liturgical assembly.

Since the Second Vatican Council, a renewed emphasis has been placed on the significance of the liturgical assembly. Within the liturgy, the assembly has its own ministerial role: to worship in spirit and in truth, to offer praise and thanksgiving to God, and to be a source of support and strength for one another. In 1977, the U.S. Bishops' Committee on the Liturgy made the bold statement that "the greatest liturgical symbol is the assembly of the Christian community transformed into the body of Christ" (NCCB Bishops' Committee 82). All ministerial roles within the liturgy serve the assembly, helping it to function in a manner that manifests the reality it is—the Body of Christ, which is the church. For this reason, any discussion of the presider's role must begin with a look at the liturgical assembly.

Historical Background for Conciliar Reform

The renewed emphasis within the church on the liturgical assembly owes a great debt to the European liturgical movements that preceded the Second Vatican Council. The liturgists of the French school, in particular, had a significant impact on Conciliar and post-Conciliar reform.[1] The work of these scholars was characterized by a careful study of the church's liturgical traditions and by a pastoral concern for the church's life of worship. This pastoral concern helped to turn the focus of the liturgical movement toward the liturgical assembly.

A key figure in this movement, Aimé-Georges Martimort, argued that both the concept and practice of assembling had undergone significant decline over the centuries. With the conviction that the twentieth-century church had lost a sense of the intimate connection between the liturgical assembly and what it means to be church, Martimort set out to retrieve a sense of the tradition of the assembly (*Introduction to the Liturgy* 77-106).

Recalling the biblical tradition of the *Qahal Yahweh*, or "assembly of Yahweh," Martimort saw the assembly as a sacred sign of God's presence among the people. The Old Testament assembly was characterized by four distinct elements:

---

1 For an overview of the pre-Conciliar scholarship on the liturgical assembly, see Vincie, "Liturgical Assembly in Magesterial and Theological Literature," 8-121.

1. It was convoked by God.

2. When the community gathered, God was in their midst.

3. God spoke a living word in the assembly.

4. The gathering ended in covenant sacrifice.

Martimort viewed the assembly within the Old Testament as a foreshadowing of the church, the assembly of the new people of God. This new assembly is convoked by Christ, who sends his heralds to proclaim the Word in the gathering of the church. Since the church is itself the Body of Christ, Head and members, the very act of gathering is a manifestation of God's presence. Here, the new covenant is sealed in blood, the blood of Christ poured out for the forgiveness of sin. For this reason, "the liturgical assembly is the most expressive manifestation on earth—a veritable *epiphany*—of the Church" (80).

As he began to look at the early traditions of the church, Martimort noted that the community had come together for prayer since the very beginning of the church's history. Gathering for worship was a hallmark of the Christian community. Moreover, liturgical prayers were always formulated in the plural.[2] This, Martimort asserted, emphasizes that the presider speaks in the name of all gathered or is involved in a dialogue with the people. The people surround the altar; it is for them that the Word of God is read. The presider designates them as offering with him the eucharistic sacrifice. Because of all these traditional characteristics of communal worship, Martimort contended that the most basic element of liturgy is undoubtedly the assembly, the gathering of the people.

As a sign, or epiphany, of the church, the liturgical assembly is the church in action, the church becoming itself and expressing the fullness of its being. It is through the liturgical assembly that the church lives out its mission of gathering all people into one. Therefore, the

---

2 "...with the exception of the biblical formulas and specifically private prayers as, at Mass, the *mea culpa*" (80).

liturgical assembly is not an optional gathering of the church but a gathering that is essential to its very existence.

This liturgical gathering is not reserved to a spiritual elite. Rather, it must gather together all God's people. In this gathering, all are called to participate. Martimort notes that active participation must be intelligent, devout, and interior. It demands a religious attentiveness. "The right and duty which the faithful have of taking an active part in the liturgy is founded on the sacrament of baptism, whose character, according to St. Thomas Aquinas' teaching, deputes one for divine worship" (89). It follows that in the liturgical assembly there are no spectators, only participants.

Another scholar who studied the assembly in biblical theology was Thierry Maertens. His work suggested a significant development in the concept of the assembly from the Old to the New Testament. Maertens emphasized the association between the assembly and the risen Lord, who seeks to unite all things in himself. The risen Christ introduces a new kind of assembly centered around himself, not localized in the Temple. Gathered in spirit and in truth, the people listen to the Word and share the meal. They are then sent on mission, which is to share the Good News of Jesus Christ and to invite others into the assembly of God's people. The early Christian assembly was further characterized by the relationship of the liturgy to the daily life of the community; i.e., the liturgy both forms and expresses the life of the faith community. Lastly, Maertens emphasized the liturgical assembly as an image of the final assembly of all God's faithful in heaven (see *Assembly for Christ*).

Summarizing the contributions of these and other scholars of the pre-Vatican II period, Catherine Vincie notes three major areas of focus in their work preceding the Council.

- The first was to clarify how the liturgical assembly and its worship related to the life of the church. Several scholars pursued and developed the concept of the liturgical assembly as a sign of the church.

- A second issue was to clarify the characteristics of the assembly, including its communal nature and the corporate nature of liturgical prayer. All are called to active but differentiated participation. Not all do the same thing, but all have essential roles in the liturgy.

- Third, this pre-Conciliar work explored the presence of Christ in the liturgical assembly and in its actions ("Liturgical Assembly: Review and Reassessment" 133).

A retrieval of the biblical sense of the assembly allowed Martimort, Maertens, and other scholars of the European liturgical movement to recover the assembly's significance and centrality in the liturgy. Both the Conciliar and post-Conciliar reforms reflect the influence of their work by upholding the liturgical assembly as a primary liturgical symbol.

Conciliar and Post-Conciliar Reform

Beginning with *Constitution on the Sacred Liturgy* and continuing through many of the liturgical documents published since the Second Vatican Council, a growing awareness of the assembly as a primary liturgical symbol is apparent. A brief review of a number of these documents will help to illustrate this fundamental point.

Constitution on the Sacred Liturgy

Constitution on the Sacred Liturgy (CSL), the first document of the Second Vatican Council to be published, began with a statement of several goals of the Council. Listed first among these was the desire to "impart an ever increasing vigor to the Christian life of the faithful" (CSL 1). One of the ways the Council sought to do this was by emphasizing the preeminence of the liturgy among the works of the church. The Council highlighted the liturgy as the summit toward which all the activity of the church is directed and the source from which the church's power flows (CSL 10). In light of the importance of the liturgy, the Council called for the participation of all God's people in the liturgy. This full, conscious, and active participation is the aim to be considered before all else in the reform and promotion of the liturgy (CSL 14). As a result, the Council called for the revision of liturgical rites and texts that would promote the role of the faithful within the liturgy (CSL 31).

General Instruction of the Roman Missal

General Instruction of the Roman Missal (GIRM) was written to introduce the Order of Mass promulgated in 1969. In addition to describing the structure of the eucharistic celebration, GIRM also offers an explanation of the doctrinal teachings that undergird the framework and celebration of the Mass. One of the concepts that forms the basis for a theology of the assembly is the royal priesthood of believers. This document makes clear that the celebration of the Eucharist is the action of the whole church, the people of God, purchased by Christ's blood, gathered together by the Lord, and nourished by his Word (GIRM 5). This assembly of God's people, made holy by sharing in the mystery of the Eucharist, is itself a sign of Christ's presence in the church.[3]

A thorough reading of GIRM clearly demonstrates the Council's emphasis upon the proper role of the people of God in the celebration

---

3 GIRM states: "For at the celebration of Mass, which perpetuates the sacrifice of the cross, Christ is really present to the assembly gathered in his name; he is present in the person of his minister, in his own word, and indeed substantially and permanently under the eucharistic elements" (GIRM 7). In her doctoral dissertation, Catherine Vincie argues that the phrase "Christ's presence in the assembly" is mistranslated from the Latin text as "Christ's presence to the assembly" in the official English translation of the GIRM as found in *Documents on the Liturgy, 1963-1979*. Vincie suggests that the Latin text better reflects Christ's presence in the assembly as one of the specifications of Christ's more general presence to the church: *In Missae enim celebratione, in qua sacrificium perpetuatur, Christus realiter praesens adest in ipso coetu in nomine suo congregato, in persona ministri, in verbo suo, et quidem substantialiter et continenter sub speciebus eucharisticus* ("Liturgical Assembly: Review and Reassessment" 152).

of the Mass. After describing the prayers and parts assigned to the priest, who presides over the assembly, GIRM next describes the dialogic nature of the celebration and the importance of the people taking part in the prayers and roles assigned to them (GIRM 14-19). Later, the document specifically describes the office and function of the people of God:

> In the celebration of the Mass the faithful are a holy people, a people God has made his own, a royal priesthood: they give thanks to the Father and offer the victim, not only through the hands of the priest, but also together with him and learn to offer themselves. They should endeavor to make this clear by their deep sense of reverence for God and their charity toward all who share with them in the celebration.
>
> They therefore are to shun any appearance of individualism or division, keeping before their mind that they have the one Father in heaven and therefore are all brothers and sisters to each other.
>
> They should become one body, whether by hearing the word of God, or joining in prayers and song, or above all by offering the sacrifice together and sharing together in the Lord's table. There is a beautiful expression of this unity when the faithful maintain uniformity in their actions and in standing, sitting, or kneeling (GIRM 62).

In expounding upon the nature of the assembly's role and its relationship to the presider, GIRM upholds the centrality of the community of believers. Sharing in the royal priesthood of Christ, the faithful are called to full participation in the eucharistic sacrifice. As an expression of their membership in the Body of Christ, that participation is characterized by a spirit of unity and service.

Directory for Masses with Children

Directory for Masses with Children (DMC), prepared and published in 1973 by the Congregation for Divine Worship, also focuses attention on the assembly. This document was written for use in planning and celebrating the liturgy with children of catechetical age. It offers guidelines and principles for adapting the liturgy to children, so that they might learn to take a more conscious and active part as members of the eucharistic assembly.

The document first addresses issues concerning the presence of children at Masses that are primarily attended by adults:

> ...in Masses of this kind it is necessary to take great care that
> the children present do not feel neglected because of their
> inability to participate or to understand what happens and what
> is proclaimed in the celebration. Some account should be taken
> of their presence... (DMC 17).

The document suggests that children be addressed in the introductory comments at the beginning of Mass or at some point in the homily. Doing so serves to provide them with a heightened sense of inclusion in the assembly.

A separate celebration of the Liturgy of the Word with the children, including a homily, is also appropriate. In this case, the children would leave the larger assembly, listen to and reflect upon the Word of God in another room, and return to the larger community before the eucharistic liturgy begins (DMC 17).

In Masses primarily attended by children, the priest and those preparing the liturgy are encouraged to adapt the words and signs so that children can more easily understand and participate in the celebration of Mass:

> The principles of active and conscious participation are in a
> sense even more significant for Masses celebrated with
> children. Every effort should therefore be made to increase this
> participation and make it more intense (DMC 22).

It is important to keep in mind that children are to participate first and foremost as members of the assembly. At times, they may also participate by cantoring, singing in the choir, proclaiming the readings, or announcing the general intercessions. When children exercise one of the specialized liturgical ministries, however, great care should be taken to see that they receive the proper liturgical formation to understand their role and the training to carry it out effectively.

DMC emphasizes the importance of including children in the celebration of the Eucharist in keeping with the primacy of the entire liturgical assembly. It encourages adaptations within the liturgy to make it more understandable to children, thus enhancing their degree of participation and forming the basis for their ongoing involvement in the life of the church.

Music in Catholic Worship

Music in Catholic Worship (MCW), a document issued in 1972 by the U.S. Bishops' Committee on the Liturgy, begins with a theology of celebration that is rooted in the liturgical assembly:

> We are Christians because through the Christian community
> we have met Jesus Christ, heard his word in invitation, and
> responded to him in faith. We gather at Mass that we may hear
> and express our faith again in this assembly and, by expressing
> it, renew and deepen it (1).

Noting the relationship between faith and the worship of the assembly, MCW states that:

> Faith grows when it is well expressed in celebration. Good
> celebrations foster and nourish faith. Poor celebrations may
> weaken and destroy it (6).[4]

For this reason, celebrations must intentionally nourish the faith of the assembly. This involves careful planning and preparation on the part of those responsible for the worship of the community.

---

4 The original text of paragraph 6 makes an even stronger statement about the relationship between poor celebrations and faith: "Faith grows when it is well expressed in celebration. Good celebrations foster and nourish faith. Poor celebrations weaken and destroy it."

In a separate section on the assembly, MCW recalls the words of GIRM that stress the importance of choosing texts, readings, prayers, and songs that correspond to the needs, religious dispositions, and attitudes of the participants (MCW 15; GIRM 313). Noting the diversity of the community, MCW directs those who plan the liturgy to be aware of the "general makeup of the total community" (17).

As it begins to address the place of music in the liturgical celebration, MCW speaks of the ministerial function of music in service to the assembly:

> ...Music should assist the assembled believers to express and share the gift of faith that is within them and to nourish and strengthen their interior commitment of faith. It should heighten the texts so that they speak more fully and more effectively. The quality of joy and enthusiasm which music adds to community worship cannot be gained in any other way. It imparts a sense of unity to the congregation and sets the appropriate tone for a particular celebration (23).

MCW then discusses the need to evaluate a given musical element for its appropriateness in a liturgical celebration. It suggests that the value of a musical piece should be evaluated from three perspectives: musical, liturgical, and pastoral. In making the liturgical and pastoral judgments in particular, the assembly must be considered:

> Music for the congregation must be within its members' performance capability. The congregation must be comfortable and secure with what they are doing in order to celebrate well (34).

MCW concludes with a statement that again emphasizes the important connection between worship and the faith of the assembly:

> There is vital interest today in the Mass as prayer, and in this understanding of the Mass lies a principle of synthesis which is essential to good liturgical worship. When all strive with one accord to make the Mass a prayer, a sharing and celebration of

Faith, the result is unity. Styles of music, choices of instruments, forms of celebration—all converge in a single purpose: that men and women of faith may proclaim and share that faith in prayer and Christ may grow among us all (84).

MCW expands and develops the sense of the assembly found in GIRM and brings the primacy of the liturgical assembly more clearly into focus.

Environment and Art in Catholic Worship

In 1978, the U.S. Bishops' Committee on the Liturgy issued a companion document to MCW that addressed the relationship of the visual arts to the liturgy. *Environment and Art in Catholic Worship* (EACW) strongly asserts that the assembly of believers is the most important liturgical symbol:

> To speak of environmental and artistic requirements in Catholic worship, we have to begin with ourselves—we who are the Church, the baptized, the initiated (27).

> Among the symbols with which the liturgy deals, none is more important than this assembly of believers... (28).

EACW also emphasizes the fact that the liturgy is the work of all the members of the community of believers:

> ...Not only the planners and ministers, however, are active in the liturgy. The entire congregation is an active component. There is no audience, no passive element in the liturgical celebration... (30).

In setting out principles for the design of church buildings, EACW once again focuses on the primacy of the assembly:

> Such a space acquires a sacredness from the sacred action of the faith community which uses it. As a place, then, it becomes quite naturally a reference and orientation point for believers. The historical problem of the Church as a *place* attaining a

> dominance over the faith community need not be repeated as
> long as Christians respect the primacy of the living assembly
> (41).

Like MCW, EACW expands the sense of the assembly found in GIRM. It suggests a theology of the assembly that is central to the liturgical celebration: the primacy of the assembly must be reflected in the very spaces that are set apart for worship.

Fulfilled in Your Hearing:
The Homily in the Sunday Assembly

Fulfilled in Your Hearing (FIYH) grew out of the U.S. bishops' concern for the quality of liturgical preaching. In 1979, the National Conference of Catholic Bishops authorized the Bishops' Committee on Priestly Life and Ministry to address the issue of the Sunday homily. As the full title of this document suggests, the assembly is to be given primary consideration in the preparation and delivery of the homily. Again, the starting point is the assembly. The homily, like the music and environment for the liturgy, must serve the assembly's centrality as a liturgical symbol. Of special note here is the very beginning of the document's discussion on the homily:

> We believe that it is appropriate, indeed essential, to begin this
> treatment of the Sunday homily with the assembly rather than
> with the preacher or the homily… (4).

The document continues by recognizing the people of God, the assembly, as the nucleus of the church and of liturgical celebration:

> …The church, therefore, is first and foremost a gathering of
> those whom the Lord has called into a covenant of peace with
> himself. In this gathering, as in every other, offices and
> ministries are necessary, but secondary. The primary reality is
> Christ in the assembly, the People of God (5).

This document is a powerful statement on the interrelationship between the presider, who is usually the preacher, and the assembly.

The bishops urge the homilist to be faithful to both the Scriptures and the community to whom they are preached, thereby mediating the message of Christ to the assembly.

Rite of Christian Initiation of Adults

The 1988 edition of the *Rite of Christian Initiation of Adults* (RCIA) also emphasizes the primacy of the liturgical assembly. It begins by describing the process of initiation as a journey that takes place within the community of the faithful (4). Throughout the ritual text of the RCIA, the liturgical assembly is seen as the normative context for the celebration of the major rites of initiation.

The assembly itself has a ministerial role in welcoming those to be initiated and in celebrating with them the liturgical rites. During the catechumenate, the catechumens are taught to keep holy the Lord's day. They do this by gathering with the community for the Liturgy of the Word at Sunday Mass, after which they are dismissed to reflect upon the Word that has been proclaimed. After their dismissal, the assembly continues to exercise its role by praying for the catechumens in the general intercessions (RCIA 83).

The sending of the catechumens to the Rite of Election offers the local community an opportunity to support the catechumens and to assure them of the church's care and support (RCIA 107). The Rite of Election is normally celebrated on the first Sunday of Lent at a gathering of the local church with its bishop, revealing to the catechumens a broader dimension of the community of the faithful.

The celebration of the sacraments of initiation usually takes place at the Easter Vigil, when the entire church gathers to welcome new members. After baptism and confirmation, the neophytes share with the entire community in offering the sacrifice and in sharing the eucharistic meal, completing their initiation into the Body of Christ.

Throughout the entire initiation process, the rite highlights the important role of the assembly in supporting the candidates with prayer and in accompanying them on the journey to the Easter sacraments. The catechumenate teaches candidates early on that the communal gathering of the faithful is integral to the life of the church and to one's own faith development.

Sunday Celebrations in the Absence of a Priest

The most recent liturgical texts to highlight the role of the liturgical assembly are the *Directory for Sunday Celebrations in the Absence of a Priest* (DSCAP), promulgated by the Congregation for Divine Worship in 1988, and the 1994 publication of *Sunday Celebrations in the Absence of a Priest: Leader's Edition* (SCAP), prepared by the NCCB in 1989.

DSCAP grew out of the need, expressed by many conferences of bishops, for the provision of liturgical celebrations in those places where a priest is not available to celebrate the Eucharist each Sunday.[5] Similarly, the preparation of the ritual text of SCAP was based on the need for providing guidance when circumstances necessitate Sunday celebrations in the absence of a priest. The introduction of SCAP (3) begins by noting that:

> The complete liturgical celebration of Sunday is characterized by the gathering of the faithful to manifest the Church, not simply on their own initiative but as called together by God, that is, as the people of God in their organic structure, presided over by a priest, who acts in the person of Christ. Through the celebration of the liturgy of the Word the assembled faithful are instructed in the paschal mystery by the Scriptures which are proclaimed and which are then explained in the homily by a priest or deacon. And through the celebration of the liturgy of the eucharist, by which the paschal mystery is sacramentally effected, the assembly participates in the very sacrifice of Christ. (See *Directory*, no. 12).

---

5 This issue of Sunday worship in the absence of a priest is a serious concern for many in the church today because it seems to threaten the place of Sunday Eucharist as the foundation of the community's life. For a thorough review of the issues at stake, see Dallen and Hughes, "Sunday Worship, " 45-57.

Word and sacrament are celebrated in the assembly of God's faithful. Yet, in certain areas, the faithful are not able to celebrate the Eucharist because of the shortage of ordained priests. When this is the case, SCAP indicates that it is still of paramount importance for the community to gather together for worship:

> ...If, in the judgment of the diocesan bishop, it is not practical or possible for the community to participate in the celebration of Mass in a church nearby (see *Directory*, no. 18), they should assemble for Sunday worship in their own community under the leadership of the person the bishop and pastor have designated to lead them in prayer... (10).

In describing the different forms that Sunday worship may take in the absence of a priest, SCAP highlights the importance of the proclamation of the Word of God and also makes provision for the sharing of holy communion (25-26). However, even when it is not possible for the faithful to receive holy communion, SCAP 26 notes that "those present should be made to realize that, nevertheless, Christ is truly present in the gathered assembly and in the Scriptures that are proclaimed. (See Vatican Council II, Constitution on the Liturgy *Sacrosanctum Concilium*, art. 7)."

By encouraging the faithful to gather for Sunday worship, even when it is not possible to share holy communion, this document clearly emphasizes the significance of the assembly. Christ is present in the assembly when the people of God gather for worship. The people of God should not be deprived of this important manifestation of Christ's presence when they are unable to participate in the celebration of Sunday Eucharist.

The Assembly As the Context for Specialized Ministry

The primacy of the assembly as a liturgical symbol has taken on increased significance in recent years. As a result, the liturgical assembly has once again become the context for both understanding and shaping all specialized liturgical ministries.

Both Martimort and Maertens noted the need for diverse functions to serve the assembly. Martimort writes that "the sharing of functions makes of the assembly an organic body, an expression of the Mystical Body of Christ (1 Cor 12:12-30), and of the liturgy a hierarchical act [with] each one playing his own role in the divinely ordered harmony of the entire action"(*Introduction to the Liturgy* 90). [6] Maertens notes that the assembly has a number of different functions: president, deacon, reader, cantor, musician, door-keeper, and commentator. Yet, "however important these duties, they are only a service of the assembly, and make it possible for all the assembly to exercise its spiritual priesthood and to express in Christ the sacrifice it is entitled to make" (Maertens 145). Chapter three of GIRM notes that specialized ministers should do all and only those functions that belong to them, highlighting the need for a variety of ministries within the liturgy. Specifically, GIRM mentions the role of the bishop, presbyter, deacon, choir, cantor, organist, acolyte, reader, special ministers of communion, servers, those who meet people at the church entrance, and those who take up the collection. Numerous books and articles have been written describing the various functions and duties of each of these ministries. But one thing remains clear: all of these ministers are to serve the assembly by helping the faithful accomplish their worship in spirit and in truth.

Robert Hovda, a leader of the liturgical renewal in the United States after Vatican II, described the assembly as the primary minister of the liturgy because the assembly is the primary sign of the priesthood of Jesus Christ. Hovda suggests that all ministry in the church, including

---

6 While championing the priesthood of the faithful and calling for greater involvement on the part of the assembly, Martimort still speaks of the hierarchical division of functions. In revising his work after the Council, Martimort shows greater sensitivity as he writes, "This differentiation of functions turns the assembly into an organic body that is the expression and manifestation of the Mystical Body of Christ, and the liturgy into a harmonious whole in which each member plays his or her proper role" (*Principles of the Liturgy* 102).

specialized liturgical ministries, depends on the assembly of God's people, on the whole church. Minister, first of all, is the function, title, and description of the church. Specialized and specific ministries within and on behalf of this community of ministers arise in response to the needs of the community. Specific ministries depend on the church, not vice versa (*Primacy of the Ministry* 17).

Eugene Walsh, who published a series of booklets[7] focusing on the assembly as the primary symbol in worship, also contextualized the role of specialized liturgical ministers. He noted that neither the presider nor the other specialized ministers can effect the Mass for the assembly. It is the action of the assembly, done deliberately and with energy, that is necessary.

Focusing on the action of the assembly, Walsh describes three dynamics of the assembly's role at worship: the assembly gathers, listens, and responds.

- Gathering involves the art of hospitality and the creation of a sense of presence.

- Listening demands an attentive awareness to the proclamation of God's Word and the openness to hear the voice of God as God speaks within the gathered assembly.

- The response of the assembly is twofold: celebrating the eucharistic meal and going forth to witness and serve.

---

7 *The Ministry of the Celebrating Community* (1977); *A Theology of Celebration* (1977); *Giving Life: the Ministry of the Parish Sunday Assembly* (1983); *Gather! Listen! Respond! The Parish Assembly's Guide to Sunday Mass* (1985). All of the these booklets were originally published by Pastoral Arts Associates of North America, Old Hickory, Tennessee. They were reissued in 1993 by Oregon Catholic Press, Portland, Oregon, under the titles: *Spirituality: Christian Life in the World Today*; *Giving Life: Ministry of the Parish Sunday Assembly*; *Celebration: Theology, Ministry and Practice*; *Proclaiming God's Love in Word and Deed*; *Proclaiming God's Love in Song.*

In this way, Walsh makes an intimate connection between the worship of the assembly and the ongoing work of the people of God as they take leave from the assembly. Throughout the entire dynamic of the liturgy, it is the assembly, and not the specialized ministers, who are the primary focus. The specialized ministers are there to serve the needs of the community and to facilitate its mission in the world.

Summary

To understand the role of the presider, it is necessary to first understand the role of the assembly. The assembly is the primary minister of the liturgy. All specialized ministries function in relation to the gathered community. The role of the presider, and all the other specialized ministries, must be seen in this context.

2. The Ministry of the Presider

When Fr. Jim arrived at his new assignment, he was replacing a pastor who had been there for twenty-nine years. In that time a new church, social hall, and rectory had been built. There were few signs, however, that any effort had been spent on building the community. Even Fr. Jim, who did not claim to be a liturgical expert, knew something was wrong when he discovered that there were no cantors, lectors, or special ministers of the Eucharist. At his first weekend Mass in the parish, one of the ushers came up to him and said, "Break a leg, Father. The show is all yours."

For centuries, within the celebration of the liturgy, the priest's role was the most important, even to the exclusion of the people.[1] Private Masses allowed the priest to function independently of a congregation. When a congregation was present, its role was minimal. The role of the people, basically, was to assist at the priest's Mass. The presider was the focal point—literally. His actions, prayers, and communion formed the axis around which the ritual revolved.

---

1 For a description of the priest's role in the celebration of the Mass, see *Ceremonial for the Use of the Catholic Churches* 1-34.

Conciliar Reform

Much of this has changed in light of post-Conciliar reform of the liturgy. The Mass and other liturgical celebrations are now seen as communal events, symbolized in the very gathering of the assembly. As such, they are not dependent upon the actions of one person alone. There is a need for a variety of ministries to serve the assembly, and no minister should be expected to fill multiple roles. Each ministry has its own specialized function within the liturgy. With this in mind, an overview of the presider's current role within the liturgical assembly follows.

Leading by Example

A review of *Constitution on the Sacred Liturgy* (CSL) in the previous chapter showed that the role of the faithful was a primary concern in the reform and promotion of the liturgy. Since all members of the people of God are called to take an active role in the liturgy, reform of the liturgy must facilitate their full and conscious participation. CSL suggests that the presider is key to enabling the members of the assembly to take their rightful place in the liturgy as they offer their worship to God. The document notes that presiders:

> must therefore realize that when the liturgy is celebrated
> something more is required than the mere observance of the
> laws governing valid and lawful celebration; it is their duty to
> ensure that the faithful take part fully aware of what they are
> doing, actively engaged in the rite, and enriched by its effects
> (11).

According to CSL, in order to promote the liturgical instruction of the faithful and their active participation in the liturgy, those who preside must:

- "become thoroughly imbued with the spirit and power of the liturgy and make themselves its teachers" (14);

- understand the liturgy and "be aided to live the liturgical life and to share it with the faithful entrusted to their care" (18);

- promote the liturgical reform with zeal and patience, leading "not only by words but also by example" (19).

CSL suggests that those who are called to facilitate the prayer of the community must first be renewed in spirit themselves. Only then can they effectively lead and animate the prayer of the assembly.

CSL notes further that:

- communal celebrations are to be given preference over individual and private celebrations, especially with regard to the celebration of Mass (27);

- within the communal celebrations, ministry is to be shared, so that each person who has a ministry to perform does only those parts that pertain to that office by nature of the rite and principles of liturgy (28).

Not only does CSL encourage members of the faithful to assume their proper roles in the liturgy, but it also implicitly reminds presiders that they are not to take the roles that belong by right to others.

Throughout the document, the presider's role is defined as considerably more than the follower of rubrics. The presider must also foster the active and conscious participation of all the faithful. The presider must facilitate and animate the worship of the assembly by word and example, enabling others, members of the assembly as well as specific ministers, to assume their rightful place in the prayer of the church.

Serving the Assembly

General Instruction on the Roman Missal (GIRM) addresses the role of the presider in a section entitled "Offices and Ministries of Holy Orders." It begins by stating that the bishop, "either in person or through the presbyters," presides over the assembly for the celebration of Mass (59). After addressing the role of the bishop, the document describes the role of the presbyter as one of service to God and to the assembly:

> Within the community of believers, the presbyter is another who possesses the power of orders to offer sacrifice in the person of Christ. He therefore presides over the assembly and leads its prayer, proclaims the message of salvation, joins the people to himself in offering the sacrifice to the Father through Christ in the Spirit, gives them the bread of eternal life, and shares in it with them. At the eucharist he should, then, serve God and the people with dignity and humility; by his bearing and by the way he recites the words of the liturgy he should communicate to the faithful a sense of the living presence of Christ (60).

The presider is one who leads the community, yet is also one with them. While the presider directs the prayer of the assembly, the presider is also to serve God's people with dignity and humility. This implies that the presider's role is not one of domination over the assembly. Rather, presiding over the assembly is an act of service, of overseeing the many aspects of the worship of the assembly.

In performing this ministry of service within the community, the presider does not function independently. Rather, the presider is to work with others in the planning and celebration of the liturgy. GIRM describes Mass with a congregation as the "basic" or "typical" form of celebration. This form of celebration also allows for a greater number of ministers to assist the presider in leading the worship of the community (GIRM 78). Here, the presider's role is to serve the assembly by coordinating the variety of liturgical ministries.

In choosing texts for the Mass the presider serves the community by considering "the spiritual good of the assembly rather than his personal outlook" (GIRM 313). The presider's ministry must be carried out in relationship to the assembly and can never be seen in isolation from the praying community.

Today, even the form of Mass without a congregation discourages the celebration of Mass by the presider alone. The presider is to be assisted by a server who makes the responses (GIRM 209) and takes the people's part to the extent possible (GIRM 210). Despite the of a congregation, the presider's role is still seen in relation to the community through the participation of at least one other member of the faithful.

Knowing the Community

In describing the offices and ministries within Masses with children, *Directory for Masses with Children* (DMC) also addresses the role of the presider. This document is more explicit than CSL or GIRM in describing the relationship between the presider and the assembly gathered for worship:

> It is the responsibility of the priest who celebrates with children to make the celebration festive, familial, and meditative. Even more than in Masses with adults, the priest is the one to create this kind of attitude, which depends on his personal preparation and his manner of acting and speaking with others.
>
> The priest should be concerned above all about the dignity, clarity, and simplicity of his actions and gestures. In speaking to the children he should express himself so that he will be easily understood, while avoiding any childish style of speech.
>
> The free use of introductory comments will lead children to a genuine liturgical participation, but these would be more than mere explanatory remarks.
>
> It will help him to reach the hearts of the children if the priest sometimes expresses the invitations in his own words, for example, at the penitential rite, the prayer over the gifts, the Lord's Prayer, the sign of peace, and communion (23).

DMC further describes the presider's role so that it more clearly includes the creation of an atmosphere of worship. GIRM's exhortation to teach the faithful by word and example is broadened in DMC to include the presider's personal preparation and style of celebration. While GIRM encourages the presider to adapt the introductory comments and invitations to prayer to the specific situation of the community, DMC notes that these introductory comments should touch the hearts of the assembly and so lead its members to full and active participation.

DMC takes another bold step when it states:

> With the consent of the pastor or rector of the church, one of
> the adults may speak to the children after the gospel, especially
> if the priest finds it difficult to adapt himself to the mentality of
> children (24).

It is more important that the assembly of children be led to understand the Gospel than to have the ordained presider preach the homily. The presider's role must be seen in relation to the assembly and in light of the presider's ability to facilitate the worship of the specific community gathered for the celebration of the liturgy.

The ability to adapt the liturgy to the needs of the assembly presumes not only an understanding of the liturgical rites themselves, but also an understanding of the particular assembly gathered here and now. Thus, the role of the presider is not simply to lead prayer, but to lead the prayer of the particular local community. DMC suggests that the presider can best lead the prayer of the assembly when the presider has a relationship with the particular community gathered for worship, knows its needs, and is able to adapt the liturgy to the local gathering of God's people.

Preparing and Planning the Celebration

Music in Catholic Worship (MCW) also speaks of the importance of the presider's role and draws explicit attention to the presider's personal engagement in the liturgy:

> No other single factor affects the liturgy as much as the
> attitude, style, and bearing of the celebrant: his sincere faith
> and warmth as he welcomes the worshiping community; his
> human naturalness combined with dignity and seriousness as
> he breaks the Bread of Word and Eucharist (21).

Here, MCW includes the presider's interior disposition as an important factor in the presider's role. The presider must be a person of faith who can share that faith warmly, naturally, and genuinely with the assembly. Sincerity and warmth, however, are not enough to make an effective presider. The presider also needs to understand the structure and theology of the rites and to invest time and energy in the thoughtful planning and preparation of the liturgical celebration.

MCW 22 stresses the importance of the presider's preparation with regard to music in the liturgy:

> The style and pattern of song ought to increase the
> effectiveness of a good celebrant. His role is enhanced when he
> is capable of rendering some of his parts in song, and he should
> be encouraged to do so. What he cannot sing well and
> effectively he ought to recite. If capable of singing, he ought,
> for the sake of the people, to rehearse carefully the sung parts
> that contribute to their celebration (Instruction on Music in the
> Liturgy, No. 8).

GIRM notes that such a degree of preparation is required in all aspects of the presider's role, especially in working with other ministers to ensure the effective celebration of the liturgy (73).

Creating an Atmosphere for Worship

There are only a few instances in *Environment and Art in Catholic Worship* (EACW) that refer specifically to the role of the presider. However, in view of the presider's role of liturgical leadership, several implications can be drawn regarding the role of presider.

EACW notes that liturgy flourishes in a climate of hospitality. Given the presider's role in facilitating the prayer of the community, it would seem to follow that the presider needs to foster this climate of hospitality so that liturgy might flourish, and that all in the assembly might be "involved as participants and *not* as spectators" (11).

The document further notes that liturgical "renewal requires the opening up of our symbols, especially the fundamental ones of bread and wine, water, oil, the laying on of hands, until we can experience all of them as authentic and appreciate their symbolic value" (15). The presider has a vital role in opening up the symbols to deepen and enhance the assembly's experience of worship.

The presider needs to be able to work with others who are experts in the field of the arts to ensure quality and appropriateness in the selection and use of liturgical vessels and vestments (EACW 93-97), and in the best use of liturgical space (EACW 39-54). By coordinating the talents of experts and the efforts of all who assist in liturgical planning, the presider works to ensure the integrity of the worship of the community. The presider seeks to ensure a harmonious unity of all the individual parts of the liturgy.

Describing the action of the liturgical assembly, EACW notes that the liturgy celebrates the in-breaking of the kingdom of God as the community seeks to put aside all barriers and discover what is common to all believers:

> ...The commonality here seeks the best which people can
> bring together rather than what is compromised or less noble.
> For the assembly seeks its own expression in an atmosphere
> which is beautiful, amidst actions which probe the entire
> human experience. This is what is most basic and most noble.
> It is what the assembly seeks in order to express the heart of
> the Church's liturgy (32).

Given the presider's role of leadership within the assembly, the presider has a special responsibility to help the members of the community discover and celebrate their common bonds within the liturgy. On the part of the presider, this implies a sensitivity to liturgy's climate as one of "awe, mystery, wonder, reverence, thanksgiving and praise" (EACW 34).

EACW also notes that worship is not simply an act of the intellect, but one that involves the total person. For this reason

> it is critically important for the Church to reemphasize a more
> total approach to the human person by opening up and

developing the non-rational elements of liturgical celebration:
the concerns for feelings of conversion, support, joy,
repentance, trust, love, memory, movement, gesture, wonder
(35).

The leader of the community's worship, the presider, needs to have a special awareness of and sensitivity to these feelings in both the self and others.

Finally, EACW 56 acknowledges the presider's influence on the community with regard to personal gestures in the liturgy:

> The liturgy of the Church has been rich in a tradition of ritual movement and gestures. These actions, subtly, yet really, contribute to an environment which can foster prayer or which can distract from prayer. When the gestures are done in common, they contribute to the unity of the worshiping assembly. Gestures which are broad and full in both a visual and tactile sense, support the entire symbolic ritual. When the gestures are done by the presiding minister, they can either engage the entire assembly and bring them into an even greater unity, or if done poorly, they can isolate. (The *Directory for Masses with Children*...bases the importance of the development of gestures, postures and actions in the liturgy on the fact that liturgy, by its nature, is the activity of the entire person [see EACW 33].)

Here, EACW suggests that the presider's role is to foster this participation in body and spirit in a way that unites the assembly in its common prayer.

Breaking Open the Word

As noted in the previous chapter, the assembly of believers is the starting point for the presentation on the homily at Sunday liturgy in *Fulfilled in Your Hearing*. It is the liturgical assembly that is the context for the ministry of the preacher. It is the assembly that helps to shape the role of the preacher.

The focus of FIYH is the Sunday homily as preached by the bishop or priest who presides at the celebration of the Eucharist. Although it recognizes other instances when the homily may be preached by someone other than the presider, it notes that:

> in terms of common practice and of liturgical norm, the
> preaching of the homily belongs to the presiding minister. (See
> *The General Instruction of the Roman Missal*, # 42: "The
> homily should ordinarily be given by the celebrant.") The unity
> of Word and Sacrament is thus symbolized in the person of the
> presiding minister of the Eucharist (Introduction).

Since the preacher is normally the presider, then, what is said about the preacher's relationship to the assembly would also apply to the homilist-presider. Describing the preacher's relationship to the assembly, FIYH notes that:

> The person who preaches in the context of the liturgical
> assembly is thus a mediator, representing both the community
> and the Lord... (12).

> The preacher represents this community by voicing its
> concerns, by naming its demons, and thus enabling it to gain
> some understanding and control of the evil which afflicts it. He
> represents the Lord by offering the community another word, a
> word of healing and pardon, of acceptance and love... (13).

> The community that gathers Sunday after Sunday comes
> together to offer God praise and thanksgiving, or at least to
> await a word that will give a meaning to their lives and enable
> them to celebrate Eucharist. What the preacher can do best of
> all at this time and in this place is to enable this community to
> celebrate by offering them a word in which they can recognize
> their own concerns and God's concern for them (14).

> The preacher acts as a mediator, making connections between
> the real lives of people who believe in Jesus Christ but are not
> always sure what difference faith can make in their lives, and

the God who calls us into ever deeper communion with
himself and with one another. Especially in the Eucharistic
celebration, the sign of God's saving presence among his
people, the preacher is called to point to the signs of God's
presence in the lives of his people so that, in joyous recognition
of that presence, they may join the angels and saints to
proclaim God's glory and sing with them their unending hymn
of praise (15).

FIYH describes the preacher, and by implication the homilist-
presider, as the mediator of meaning as the presider ministers within
the assembly. The homilist-presider does this in a particular way
through the homily, but this role is not limited to the homily alone.
The preacher who helps the members of the assembly discover
meaning in their lives through the homily is ordinarily the same person
who leads the community in offering their worship to God. In both
preaching the homily and leading the prayer of the community, the
homilist-presider mediates meaning and helps the people to reflect
upon the Word of God, to make the connection between their lives
and their relationship in faith with God, and then to offer their prayer
of worship to God.

Just as preachers who are conscious of their role "strive to preach
in a way that indicates they know and identify with the people to whom
they are speaking," homilist-presiders must lead the worship of the
assembly in a manner that indicates they know and identify with the
people whom they lead in worship. Presiding, like preaching, must be
pastoral, "displaying a sensitive and concerned knowledge of the
struggles, doubts, concerns, and joys of the members of a local
community" (FIYH 18). In order to know and identify with the people,
FIYH notes that

the preacher will have to be a listener before he is a speaker.
Listening is not an isolated moment. It is a way of life. It
means openness to the Lord's voice not only in the Scriptures
but in the events of our daily lives and in the experience of our

> brothers and sisters. It is not just *my* listening but *our* listening
> together for the Lord's Word to the community... (20).

In order to open up God's Word to the community, the preacher needs to listen to that Word and to the words of the community. In a similar way, the homilist-presider needs to listen to both the voice of God in Scripture and to the voices of the people who make up the particular assembly.

Preachers also need a knowledge of history and a familiarity with the complex social, political, and economic forces that shape the contemporary world in order to be effective in their ministry:

> ...Without this kind of informed understanding of the complex
> world we live in, preaching too easily degenerates into
> platitudes of faith, meaningless broadsides against the
> wickedness of the modern world, or into an uncritical
> affirmation of the wonderful advances that have taken place in
> modern times (FIYH 34).

The homilist-presider is one who serves the assembly by openness to the Word of God and to the voices of the assembly. As the preacher needs to be sensitive to the concerns and needs of the community in the preparation and delivery of the homily, so, too, the presider needs to attend to the cares and concerns of the community as the presider enables the assembly to offer its great prayer of thanksgiving to God.

Contemporary Reflections on the Ministry of the Presider

Since the Second Vatican Council, a number of contemporary liturgists have begun to reflect on the presider's ministry in light of the presider's relationship to the liturgical assembly. A review of several authors who have explored this relationship follows.

Facilitating an Experience of Church

Describing the role of the presider, Robert Hovda writes, "The presider is *in, of, by,* and *for the church,* and the church is the liturgical assembly" ("For Presiders/Preachers" 28). He develops this statement in his book *Strong, Loving and Wise,* published as a manual for presiders. Drawing on the ideas and experiences of many pastoral practitioners and many congregations who have participated in the renewal of the liturgy since Vatican II, Hovda develops a theology of presiding that is situated within the context of the liturgical assembly (vii).

As intimated in both CSL and GIRM, Hovda describes the ministry of presiding as a service of leadership within the assembly. He notes further that:

> As "a service of leadership," it normally assumes an already
> existing relationship with the community assembled.
> Ordinarily one should not be leading people in an activity as
> deep and central and personal as their ritualizing about the
> meaning of their lives unless one has previously known them
> and served them in a role related to fundamental issues (8).

Hovda emphasizes the relationship of trust that must exist between the presider and the assembly in the planning, preparation, and celebration of the liturgy. The presider can function most effectively in this ministry of service if the presider knows the community and shares its life. This kind of relationship can help the presider in expressing the assembly's most basic needs before God. He writes:

> When we realize clearly that our entire job in presiding is
> facilitating the assembly's *experience* of church, community of
> faith, kingdom witness, men and women together as sisters and
> brothers before God without the distinctions and roles and
> categories within which they operate daily—when that
> realization takes hold, then everything we do and say and
> handle and touch in the liturgy, as well as the scene we set for
> the action, demands an attention that is greater rather than less.
> Now each element has to contribute to the experience of the

people. Each element is not simply something that has to be done. It is something that has to be done because the doing of it is meeting real human needs (47; see also MCW 21).

Here, the presider's role is to help the community understand what it means to be church. The church is the gathering of God's people who come together to praise God and to draw strength for the church's mission in the world, namely witnessing to the kingdom by a life of faith-filled service to all God's people.

Reflecting a Prayerful Presence

The ministry of presiding is a service of leadership to the community based on a relationship between the presider and the assembly. This service is expressed in the presider's attentiveness to the assembly and in a personal presence that is characterized by warmth and hospitality. Hovda notes that this personal presence is expressed in liturgical celebration through the presider's style that is "appropriate, honest, authentic, as genuine and real as it can be" (*Strong, Loving and Wise* 63; see also DMC 23).

As implied in EACW, Hovda emphasizes the need for good style in liturgy:

> In the liturgical assembly we are striving to be at the height of our God-consciousness and therefore at the height of our human-consciousness. It is an awesome thing to face the mystery of the Other and the mystery of ourselves with such clear purpose and intent. The obvious inadequacy of words and language in this enterprise makes our worship rest (even more heavily than other events do) on symbols and on style (63-64; see also EACW 56).

Because style is so important, Hovda notes that presiders need to work to become good at it. Attention to the assembly is an essential component in developing a style that is faithful to the ministry of presiding as a service of leadership within the community.

Another liturgist who sees the prayer of the assembly as the context for the ministry of presiding is Aidan Kavanagh. In *Elements of Rite: A Handbook of Liturgical Style*, he reflects on the ministry of the presider in light of the documents of the post-Conciliar reform of the liturgy. Regarding the presider as servant of the assembly he notes:

> When it gathers, the assembly stands in worship before the Creator as sacrament and servant in Christ of a new-made world. This is serious business. The liturgical minister, being part of the assembly, must think and act accordingly, being neither flippant nor dour, neither informal nor rigid. The minister, especially the one who presides, should know both the assembly and its liturgy so well that his looks, words, and gestures have a confident and easy grace about them. He presides not over the assembly but within it; he does not lead it but serves it; he is the speaker of its house of worship. His decisions must never be gratuitous. They may sometimes be wrong, but they must always be steeped in a sense of reverent pastoral responsibility that is completely infused with the assembly and its tradition of liturgical worship. The sort of ministerial discretion this requires is a high art more important than any rubric ever written—just as the artistry of a good cook is more important to human dining than any recipe ever written (12-13; see also CSL 11, 19; GIRM 60; and EACW 9, 15).

Kavanagh situates the ministry of presiding within the assembly and sees it as an act of pastoral service to the community. He describes presiding as an art and notes that, "It is achieved under grace by constant prayer, reflection, self-discipline, and continuing practice on the minister's part" (39).

Building Up the Kingdom of God

A final connection between the assembly and the ministry of the presider is made by two authors who look to the traditions of the early church in regard to liturgical presidency. Hervé-Marie Legrand looks at the ancient tradition of liturgical presidency and concludes that "the presidency of the eucharistic assembly is seen as the liturgical, prophetic, and mysteric dimension of the pastoral charge of building up the Church which is conferred in ordination" (430). For Legrand, the assembly as a whole celebrates the Eucharist. Even as the presider leads the community, the presider does so as a member of the assembly. In the early church, the presider could only lead the community's worship because he was presiding over the Christian community in its day-to-day concerns as well.

Richard Szafranski also looks to the ancient tradition of the church and draws the conclusion "that the early Christian community held that competency in leadership of the community meant competency to preside at Eucharist" (307). Szafranski notes that this essential link to the community is crucial for the ministry of community leadership. There is a fundamental relationship between the community and its leader, a relationship of trust that develops in the day-to-day life of the community (see FIYH 12-39).

Both Legrand and Szafranski raise questions about liturgical presidency in "priestless communities." Given the centrality of the Eucharist in the Roman tradition, who should preside when the community gathers to pray? Can the community celebrate the Eucharist without an ordained presbyter? Both authors seem to imply that current practice, which links eucharistic presidency to ordination more so than to pastoral leadership within the community, needs to be questioned. In suggesting that the one who provides community leadership should also be "designated" in some way to preside at the community's celebration of the Eucharist, these authors seem to imply that the presider's role must be rooted in a role of pastoral leadership within the community. This leadership is expressed in the concrete pastoral care that the presider provides within a local community on a regular basis.[2] This link between community and liturgical leadership is one

---

2 In a contemporary sociological study of the role of women pastors in some U.S. Roman Catholic parishes, Ruth Wallace argues that the reason women are accepted as pastors is precisely because of their pastoral care of the community.

further way the presider gives witness to the assembly of the intimate connection between leadership and service in building up the kingdom of God.

Summary

Within the context of the liturgical assembly, the role of the presider is one of servant leadership. The presider serves the assembly by leading the worship of the gathered community. As the one who directs the worship of the community, the presider coordinates the ministries of others in the assembly and works to foster the full, conscious, and active participation of all the people.

By the presider's own prayerful preparation and participation in the liturgy, the presider animates the worship of the assembly and leads the community to a deeper dimension of faith through its worship. The presider unfolds the symbols for the assembly, leading them into fuller communion with one another and with God.

The presider can more effectively lead the worship of the community when there is an ongoing relationship between the presider and the assembly. This sense of trust is developed in the day-to-day interaction of the presider with the community and is deepened through the presider's pastoral care for the community. By coming to know the community in its daily life, the presider leads the community in bringing to worship its joys and sorrows, its struggles and triumphs.

In addition to knowing the particular assembly that gathers for worship and their cultural context, the presider needs to know the rhythm and flow of the liturgy so as to direct the worship of the assembly in a harmonious way, in a manner that integrates the human and divine aspects of liturgy. In creating an atmosphere for worship and in breaking open God's Word, the presider must demonstrate the graciousness of God by a strong yet gentle presence.

Finally, the presider needs to develop a style of presiding that is personal and prayerful, a style that reflects the personal faith commitment of the presider. The presider's style of facilitating and animating the worship of the community must also respect others and enable them to participate fully in the celebration, and in the church's mission of building up God's kingdom.

3. Preparing to Preside

After celebrating the rite of committal at the cemetery, Helen was approached by several children of Florence, the woman who had just been buried. They told Helen what a wonderful job she had done in leading the funeral liturgy. While at first they were disappointed that Fr. Joe was not able to be with them to celebrate their mother's funeral Mass, they were now very grateful that Helen was the one to lead them in prayer. After all, Helen was the one who brought their mother communion each Sunday and who visited her regularly in the hospital. It now seemed only right that Helen was the one to preside over their mother's burial.

In preparing for the funeral rites, Helen was not certain how well she would do. After all, this was her first funeral. But she had studied the funeral rite and had chosen the prayers and readings in light of her relationship with Florence. She reflected on the readings and carefully composed the words of comfort she would speak. It was no wonder that Florence's children were grateful, for Helen had helped them to celebrate their mother's passage into the eternal life that awaits us all.

More and more pastoral ministers such as Helen are being asked to lead the prayer of the assembly in the absence of an ordained minister. As others begin to assume a ministry that was once the exclusive role of the clergy, it is important to help them gain a practical understanding of all that is involved in leading liturgical prayer. A number of considerations for those preparing to preside follow.

- By definition, *liturgy is the work of the people.* The one who presides at liturgy needs to see this ministry as an exercise of pastoral care for the people of God as they offer their worship.

- *Liturgy is the prayer of the church*; it both forms and expresses the faith of the community. Therefore, the presider needs to be attentive to the ritual nature of liturgical prayer and to understand the structure of the rites and the theology that undergirds them.

- The action of the *liturgy involves ritual communication* with God and with others. The presider has a key role in facilitating and animating this communication. The presider, therefore, must understand the different communication patterns within the liturgy and be skilled in both the verbal and nonverbal languages of the liturgy.

- *One of the goals of the liturgy is to lead the community and its members into a deeper relationship with God.* As the one charged with leading the community in its prayer, the presider, in a particular way, needs to be attentive to the growth and development of faith within the community. The presider needs to take time to reflect on the exercise of this ministry and to evaluate how effectively it facilitates the proclamation of the kingdom of God.

Presiding As Pastoral Care for the Assembly

In its basic meaning, liturgy is the work of the people. When the assembly gathers to worship, the faithful join their prayer to that of

Christ who offers a sacrifice of praise to God. In this gathering, the faithful are called to full, conscious, and active participation.

This participation is first and foremost a sharing in the dying and rising of Christ, reflected in the way the faithful hear and respond to God's call. When the members of the assembly are aware of God's presence, this sense of participation is manifested in the way the assembly celebrates its faith. To participate fully, consciously, and actively means more than going through the motions of singing and responding at liturgy. It means that the members of the community are firmly rooted in their baptismal call and in their sharing in Christ's paschal mystery. This conviction leads the members of the assembly to gather together and to celebrate their faith with zeal, conviction, and enthusiasm.

To foster this participation most effectively, the presider needs to help the assembly to see the intimate connection between the paschal mystery and the life of the community. The presider does this by both encouraging and challenging the community in the way it lives out the Gospel of Jesus Christ. The deeper a community enters into the mystery of Christ's love, and expresses that love by a commitment to evangelization and service, the more fully it will participate in authentic worship.

In order for the presider to most effectively invite the assembly into a deeper communion with God and neighbor, the presider needs to be in touch with the particular community that has gathered for worship. This knowledge is more than mere information about the community. It is an intimate knowledge that comes from investing time and energy in getting to know the members of the community. By spending time with community members, by listening to their stories, by getting involved in the issues that concern the community, the presider begins to develop a relationship of trust with the community that can make this ministry more effective.

As noted above in chapter two, sociologist Ruth Wallace makes a strong connection between community leadership and pastoral care. She asserts that, in order to shepherd the community effectively, the leader needs to be actively involved in the life of the community and to approach the community and its members with a pastoral heart. She speaks of the pastoral heart in terms of the relationship of love and care that exists between the pastor and the community. Wallace suggests three essential characteristics of the pastoral heart: calling people by name, visiting members of the community, and developing a sense of personal warmth that enables the community to see that the leader is "one of us" (47-65). Those who lead need to walk with the community on its journey of faith as it experiences joys and sorrows, triumphs and failures. In ministering to the community in its daily life, the presider learns how to minister at liturgy—with compassion, sensitivity, and a warmth that comes as a result of a personal relationship of care for the community.

Linking worship with pastoral care, pastoral theologian Elaine Ramshaw suggests that the "paradigm for presiding at the Eucharist is that of a gracious invitation: come and enter into the realm of God, where the royal banquet, the wedding feast, is spread for tax collectors and sinners, and the poor dragged in off the street" (20). Extending this invitation to the community, the presider invites the members of the assembly into a deeper relationship of love with God and with others. Part of the presider's ministry includes creating a sense of hospitality so that all feel welcome. As a minister of pastoral care, the presider needs to exercise this ministry with graciousness and hospitality so that none feel excluded.[1]

In caring for the assembly, the presider is called to follow the example of Jesus, who nurtures the life of God's Spirit within the community and its members by feeding them with the bread of God's Word and the bread of the Eucharist. By walking with the community and responding to their needs with a pastoral heart, the presider comes to know the physical, spiritual, and emotional hungers of the commu-

---

1 Ramshaw notes that, within the liturgy, children are often excluded from the worship of the community. Here, the presider needs to develop the ability to welcome and include all, young and old alike (39-41). Others who are often excluded from the community's worship are persons who have significant developmental disabilities. For a fuller discussion of this issue, see Harrington.

nity. As one who cares for the people of God, the presider must also work to facilitate the community's response to those who are in need, so that both its worship and its daily life might reflect a full participation in the paschal mystery, the dying and rising of Christ.

The presider should reflect on some important questions with regard to this particular gathering of God's people when preparing to preside:

- Who are the members of the assembly that I am called to lead?

- What is my relationship with this community?

- How do I know and respond to the joys and sorrows of this community?

- How am I sensitive to its issues and concerns?

- What is God asking me to share with this community as I lead it in prayer?

- How does the worship of the assembly reflect the community's daily living of the Gospel?

Such questions can help to turn the heart and mind of the presider toward the assembly and allow the community's needs and issues to become a part of the worship of this local community.

Presiding over the Public Prayer of the Church

In addition to being in touch with the community gathered for prayer, the presider needs to be thoroughly familiar with the church's traditions of liturgical prayer. This implies that the presider knows the difference between liturgical prayer and devotional prayer. This also demands that the presider know the structure of liturgical prayer and the theology that undergirds the rites.

Liturgical Prayer vs. Devotional Prayer

One of the basic skills for presiding is a knowledge of the liturgical rites of the church. Before presuming that one can preside at liturgy, one must understand the distinction between liturgical and devotional prayer. Liturgical prayer is the official public prayer of the community (e.g., the Eucharist and other sacramental celebrations, Liturgy of the Hours, Liturgy of the Word, Sunday celebration in the absence of a priest, etc.). It is formal and structured and uses ritual patterns of communication. Liturgical prayer links word and gesture. It expresses the faith of the community and tends to be of a general nature. Those who are called to preside at liturgical prayer must understand that this is the official public prayer of the church. As such, there is a clearly defined structure for prayer and a specific role for the one who presides. The presider is not free to change the liturgy at whim.

Devotional prayer, on the other hand, is more personal and reflects the piety of the individual praying. It is often related to personal experience and can be structured or unstructured. It may be prayed individually or in common. But even when devotional prayer is structured and prayed in common (e.g., Stations of the Cross, the rosary, and novenas), it does not become liturgical prayer. It is not the official public prayer of the church.

The Structure and Theology of the Rites

Throughout the ages, the church has taught that there is an intimate connection between how we pray (the external structure of the rite) and the deeper meaning of the prayer (the theology of a particular rite). In other words, the way we pray reflects what we believe. To preside effectively demands that the leader of prayer know both the structure of the rites and the theology behind them.

On a very practical level, the presider needs to know the basic structure and sequence of prayer to know and anticipate what comes next in the liturgical celebration. Understanding the underlying theology helps the presider understand why things are done as they are. For example, in the structure of Mass, the Liturgy of the Word is preceded by the introductory rites. Understanding the theology of the Mass reveals that the purpose of the introductory rites is to gather the community and prepare the assembly to listen to the Word. Knowing both the structure and the theology of the Mass helps the presider to keep the introductory rites in perspective. They are what their name suggests—introductory; as such, they should be as simple and uncluttered as possible.

The structure and theology of the rites are best learned by taking time to study both the liturgical texts and the introductions to the liturgical rites as found in the church's official liturgical books. By investing time in the study of these texts, the presider can come to a better understanding of what the church intends in a particular celebration and how the structure of the rite both reflects and brings about the church's intention. For example, one of the church's intentions with regard to baptism is that it celebrates the incorporation of the person being baptized into the Body of Christ. For this reason, both the Rite of Christian Initiation of Adults and the Rite of Baptism of Children are structured to be celebrated within the context of a living faith community and not as private events, thus reflecting the communal nature of the church.

The liturgical texts and the introductions to the liturgical books are also an excellent source for personal meditation and prayer. Spending time in prayer with the liturgical texts can help to deepen the presider's spirituality so that the presider is truly an instrument of God's grace when leading the community in its common prayer.

Enactment of the Presider's Role

In addition to knowing the structure and theology of the rites, the presider needs to learn how best to put that knowledge into practice. It is one thing to know what the church intends. It is quite another to bring about this intention. The presider needs to be attentive to the enactment of the rites. For example, one knows that the greeting, "The Lord be with you," and its response, "And also with you," are meant to be a dialogue between the presider and the assembly. But in order for it to be a true dialogue, there needs to be a purposeful engagement between the presider and the people. In speaking those words, the presider needs to make eye contact with the assembly and sustain eye contact while the community makes its response. For this to be a dialogue, the presider cannot be looking at the text while saying the words, or be turning pages while the assembly makes its response.

As noted earlier, *Music in Christian Worship* (MCW) indicates that good liturgical celebrations strengthen and nourish faith, while poor celebrations may weaken and destroy faith. This same document also notes that no other single factor affects the liturgy as much as the attitude, style, and bearing of the presider (MCW 6; MCW 22). Together, these two statements imply that good presiders can nourish and sustain faith while poor presiders can weaken and destroy faith. For this reason, the presider needs to be attentive to the important connection between intention and enactment. Taking time to reflect on how one presides can serve to make a leader of prayer more effective in this ministry. By asking *"What* am I doing?" and *"Why* am I doing what I do?"*, the presider can examine if both word and gesture reflect what the church intends.

The presider also needs to be careful not to impose a personal spirituality upon the assembly. It may be an expression of the presider's personal spirituality to strike the breast as a gesture of humility whenever the words "Lord, have mercy" are prayed as part of the penitential rite. By adding this gesture the presider confuses a public proclamation of God's mercy with a personal expression of devotion. In addition, adding this gesture may confuse the members of the assembly by making them wonder: Why is the presider doing that? What does it mean? Are we supposed to be doing the same thing? The one who leads the prayer of the community needs to be aware that the presider's role influences the actions and attitudes of the assembly. The liturgy is not the place for the presider to add elements of personal piety that are not part of the liturgical prayer of the church.

In the role of leading prayer, the presider also needs to develop a quality of transparency so that God's grace is channeled through the presider's ministry. While the words and actions of the presider are important, what is more important is the way that the presider's words and actions manifest the presence of Christ. Here, the presider would do well to follow the message of John the Baptist, that Christ must increase while I must decrease (Jn 3:30). The presider's words and actions must always point to Christ, who offers our prayer to the Father.

In preparing to lead the public prayer of the church, the presider might reflect on the following questions:

- How do I show that I understand the difference between public prayer and devotional prayer?

- How does my manner of presiding reflect the structure of liturgical prayer? How familiar am I with the order of the particular rite I will be celebrating?

- When was the last time I read and reflected on the theology of the liturgical rites, as found in the introduction to the liturgical books?

- How well does what I do reflect the theology of the rites?

- What is the meaning of the words and gestures I use?

- How careful am I that my words and actions reflect the mind of the church?

- What elements of personal piety have I added to the public prayer of the church? How are these elements appropriate to the liturgical prayer of the church?

- How does my way of presiding draw attention to me or to Christ?

Learning the Languages of Prayer

In addition to being in touch with the assembly and knowing the structure and theology of the rites, the presider also needs to develop the skill of praying publicly in leading the worship of the assembly.

Kathleen Hughes has identified seven different patterns of communication within the liturgical celebration with which the presider needs to become familiar ("Types of Prayer in the Liturgy" 959-967):

1. nonverbal communication, including silence, gestures, and bodily attitudes;

2. the presider's formal address to the community;

3. the presider's informal address to the community;

4. the presider's personal address to God;

5. the presider's address to God in the name of the community;

6. the prayers of the presider and community in dialogue; and

7. the prayers of the presider and community in unison .

The presider needs to know and understand the difference between these types of communication so that the language of the assembly's prayer reflects the content of the church's prayer.

Nonverbal Communication

In learning the nonverbal dimensions of prayer, the presider needs to develop a sense of gracefulness in movement and reverence in gesture (Huck 46-47). *Environment and Art in Catholic Worship* (EACW) 56 notes that:

> The liturgy of the Church has been rich in a tradition of ritual movement and gestures. These actions, subtly, yet really, contribute to an environment which can foster prayer or which can distract from prayer. When the gestures are done in common, they contribute to the unity of the worshiping assembly. Gestures which are broad and full in both a visual and tactile sense, support the entire symbolic ritual. When the gestures are done by the presiding minister, they can either

engage the entire assembly and bring them into an even greater unity, or if done poorly, they can isolate. (The *Directory for Masses with Children*...bases the importance of the development of gestures, postures and actions in the liturgy on the fact that liturgy, by its nature, is the activity of the entire person [see EACW 33].)

This implies that the presider needs to learn how to make every movement a part of prayer. Walking in procession, bowing, genuflecting, making the sign of the cross, extending hands to invite the community into prayer, extending hands in the "orans"[2] position for prayer, making eye contact, and using facial expressions are all important elements in nonverbal communication.

Liturgical processions are more than opportunities for people to get from one place to another. Within the liturgy, processions symbolize the pilgrim journey of the people of God. As the procession moves through the assembly, the members of the procession represent the entire community on journey to the City of God. When the presider is walking in procession through the liturgical assembly, the presider needs to move at an unhurried pace and take time to acknowledge the presence of Christ within the assembly and its members.

For example, during the entrance procession, the presider appropriately joins the assembly in singing the entrance song. As the presider moves through the community, it is also important to make eye contact with those who have gathered, thereby acknowledging the presence of Christ within the assembly and its members. This presumes that the assembly is also conscious of its role during the entrance procession, namely, gathering as the Body of Christ, Head and members, singing a song of praise to God who is present in their midst.

Genuflecting is one way of showing reverence to the presence of Christ within the liturgical celebration. It is a gesture usually reserved for the veneration of Christ present in the eucharistic elements. When

---

2 In the "orans" position, the arms are extended outward, and the palms of the hands are turned slightly upward.

genuflecting, the presider should make the gesture in an unhurried and graceful manner, taking time to touch the right knee to the ground.

Bowing is another sign of reverence and respect. There are a number of times within the liturgy when the rubrics call for the presider to bow toward the altar or the cross. The presider can make a deep bow from the waist, or a more simple bow of the head. In either case, the gesture needs to be performed in a graceful manner.

At the beginning of the liturgy, the presider makes the sign of the cross in the traditional manner of touching the right hand to the forehead, heart, and shoulders. This is a different gesture than blessing the community with the sign of the cross. When the ordained presider blesses the people with the sign of the cross, the presider extends the right arm and hand, and traces the sign of the cross over the people. Both gestures need to be broad and full and to correspond to the words being said.

When the presider is praying with the community, as in during the Gloria, the presider's hands need to be in a position that reflects a certain comfort with prayer. Some presiders are more comfortable with folded hands, others with one hand resting on the other slightly below chest level. Each presider needs to determine what is the best position for the hands "at rest."

When the presider invites the community to prayer by saying "Let us pray," the presider extends both arms in a gracious gesture of invitation. Beginning with hands "at rest," the presider opens both arms beyond the shoulders and then brings the hands back to rest while the community takes a moment for silent prayer. The presider then extends hands in the "orans" position, extending arms beyond the shoulder and hands upward in prayer.

It is also important that the presider recognize the importance of the eyes in nonverbal communication. The presider needs to make eye contact with the assembly when addressing them, for example when saying, "The Lord be with you." It is also important for the presider to sustain eye contact with the assembly while it voices its response, such as "And also with you." Both are important elements of the communication, and the presider needs to be attentive to the assembly in both the invitation and in the response.

There are other times when it does not seem appropriate for the presider to be looking at the assembly. When voicing the prayer of the community (e.g., during the opening prayer), the presider should be looking either at the text of the prayer or focusing the gaze at some point other than the community. At other times within the liturgy, the presider needs to focus attention on the action of the liturgy (e.g., to look at the reader during the proclamation of the Word).

The presider should be conscious of the other ways that facial expression fosters communication in the liturgy. Expressing a smile or a nod of welcome during the opening procession can help to create a hospitable atmosphere for worship, just as rolling the eyes or grimacing in disgust during a lector's poor proclamation of the Word can disrupt the spirit of prayer. The presider needs to be conscious of the fact that presiding is a public role, and the assembly looks to the presider as a leader and role model.

To be at ease with the ritual gestures and movements of the liturgy implies that the presider is comfortable with the human body and that the presider sees the entire body as an important element in leading prayer. Eugene Walsh notes that:

> Worship is a human experience, not a set of concepts. It is a
> thing of beauty and warmth. It is a body-thing, not a
> head-thing. There is no way for one to think oneself into being
> a good presider. One has got to get it into one's muscles and
> bones, just like dancers, actors, and ballplayers (6).

Another nonverbal dimension of prayer that is important in liturgical celebration is silence. Silence is more than the absence of words. It is a stillness that enables the community to hear and reflect upon the Word of God. It is a time that allows the human spirit to communicate more deeply with the Spirit of God. For this reason, times for silence should never be rushed. The Foreword to *General Instruction on the Roman Missal* (GIRM) notes that:

> The proper use of periods of silent prayer and reflection will
> help to render the celebration less mechanical and impersonal
> and lend a more prayerful spirit to the liturgical rite.

The presider needs to become comfortable with silence and to help create an appropriate rhythm and pace to the liturgy by its use.

Verbal Communication

Just as the presider needs to cultivate the skills of nonverbal communication in the liturgy, the skills of leading the spoken and sung prayers of the liturgy also need to be developed. The presider needs to learn how to proclaim the ritual texts. Gabe Huck suggests that:

> Grace and reverence are important here also: how are they
> found in the tone, volume, pace and cadences of the speech?
> Much of what the presider speaks, especially in the eucharistic
> prayers, are familiar words. The challenge is not to find a way
> to make them sound somehow new each time, but rather to
> find a way of speaking that fits this occasion of great
> thanksgiving (47).

In speaking the prayers of the liturgy, the presider needs to find the appropriate tone of voice that reinforces the words that are spoken, and to adapt the voice to the proportion of the worship space and the size of the community. However, by projecting the voice so that all can hear clearly, the prayer leader also needs to be careful that the presider's voice does not drown out the assembly. As the presider learns how to pray publicly, a sense of timing needs to be developed when entering into dialogue with the praying community. The presider needs to keep the liturgy moving while at the same time giving the members of the community ample time to respond. The presider also has to learn to give the community appropriate cues that lead into the assembly's responses.

In addition to learning how to use tone of voice, volume, scale, timing, rhythm, and verbal cues in leading the prayer of the community, the presider also needs to learn how to improvise and how to adapt the informal introductions to prayer. Here the presider needs to be attentive so that improvisation does not turn prayers and their introductions into mini-homilies or verbose exhortations. Rather, the presider needs to prepare carefully beforehand the adaptations to the texts, using an economy of words.

The presider must also be prepared to deal with the unexpected in the liturgy. In the words of liturgist Edward Foley, it is a matter of "acknowledging the bull in the china shop." If the bride faints during the wedding liturgy, or if one of the mourners at a funeral liturgy is wailing unceasingly, the presider must be able to respond to the situation with sensitivity and compassion, and not pretend that nothing out of the ordinary has happened. Here the presider needs to remember that liturgy is never perfect. Despite the best intentions, there will be distractions and interruptions that are beyond the presider's control. The presider needs to learn how best to respond as Christ would in this particular situation.

As one who serves the assembly by leading its prayer, the presider needs to learn the skill of leading public prayer in both its verbal and nonverbal dimensions. The presider needs to coordinate both dimensions of public prayer so that there is a harmony between word and action. Here too, the presider needs to be comfortable with the structure and the flow of the liturgy, so that both words and actions serve to facilitate the prayer of the gathered community. In this regard, the presider might reflect on the following questions:

- How does my style of presiding show that I understand the power of both the spoken and unspoken word?

- How do my words echo the Word of God?

- How careful am I to use an economy of words when making spontaneous comments?

- How do I respond to distractions within the liturgy?

- How graceful are my movements and gestures?

- How well do my words and gestures correspond?

- How do I incorporate periods of silence into the liturgy?

- How do I live the words of the liturgy?

- How faithfully do I pray and reflect on the prayers I am called to proclaim?

The Skill of Working with Others

Because the presider's role is situated within the context of a praying community, the presider needs to develop the skill of working with others. One model for working with others has been proposed by James and Evelyn Whitehead in their writing on collaborative ministry. They suggest the concept of partnership as an example of how ministers can work together:

> Partnership, both in the Gospel and in contemporary life, is an experience of shared power. In this communal process, we explicitly reject domination of one by the other. Being partners does not mean that we bring the same thing to our relationship or that each of us contributes equally....Partners recognize that their differences often expand and enrich their relationships.... Partnership depends on mutuality. The giving and receiving go both ways. In a mutual relationship, each party brings something of value; each receives something of worth. Partnership thrives when we recognize and respect this mutual exchange of gifts (*Promise of Partnership* 8).

The Whiteheads propose the model of a partnership as an image of collaborative ministry that respects the uniqueness of each individual and the gifts that each person brings to the relationship. The partnership model highlights the presider's role as servant, who leads the community's worship but does not dominate in directing the assembly and the other liturgical ministers. Similarly, such a partnership enables the presider to lead the prayer of the community while at the same time encouraging all the members of the community to assume their rightful places within the liturgy.

As partner to all other members within the liturgy, the presider needs to be careful not to show favoritism to groups or individuals within the liturgy. For example, if the presider cannot call each person in the assembly by name when distributing communion, the presider should not call anyone by name, lest some feel excluded at the very moment that signifies union with and in the Body of Christ. The presider's role demands a sense of inclusivity and hospitality toward all.

The partnership model should also be reflected in other relational aspects of the presider's ministry outside the liturgy. In the presider's daily life, the presider needs to work in close relationship with others. Both in coming to know the concerns of the community and in fostering the community's response to those in need, the presider needs to know how to work with others as partners to make the best use of the gifts and talents of others for the good of the community.

Here, the presider might reflect on the following questions:

- How well do I work with others in the planning
  and celebration of the liturgy?

- How do I promote and facilitate other liturgical ministries?

- How do I animate the assembly to full, conscious,
  and active participation?

- How do my relationships outside the liturgy affect
  my style of presiding within the liturgy?

- How do I help the members of the assembly feel
  welcome and included within the liturgy?

The Skill of Theological Reflection

The final skill to be considered is that of theological reflection. *Constitution on the Sacred Liturgy* (CSL) specifies that presiders "are to be helped by every suitable means to understand more fully what it is they are doing in their liturgical functions" (18). Understanding the liturgy means more than knowing the rubrics (CSL 11). Rather, the presider must become imbued with the power and spirit of the liturgy (CSL 14) so that he or she can lead the faithful to take part in the liturgy, fully aware of what they are doing, actively engaged in the rite, and enriched by its effects (CSL 11).

A number of contemporary theologians have begun to explore the relationship between ministry and theological reflection. The White-heads suggest that "effective ministry is and has been the result of an ongoing dynamic of reflection and action" (*Method in Ministry* 1). They propose both a method and a model for theological reflection with the goal of helping ministers to serve more faithfully and effectively. James Poling and Donald Miller emphasize the need for critical and constructive reflection if ministry is to be faithful to its task of building up God's kingdom for all persons (12). Don Browning emphasizes the need for a minister to be a "reflective practitioner," one who can not only act, but also reflect upon one's actions (3). Thomas Groome describes an approach to ministry called "shared Christian praxis" that includes critical reflection as a key moment in the process (333). These authors suggest that the "doing" of ministry, when accompanied by a process of critical reflection, can lead to a renewed and more effective ministry. The ministry of presiding is most effective when accompanied by the process of theological reflection.

As the presider ministers within the liturgical assembly, he or she needs to reflect critically on the experience of presiding. Knowing the details of how to preside is one thing. Being able to facilitate the assembly's ongoing transformation into the Body of Christ is another. The presider needs to learn how to evaluate the role of presiding in this ongoing process.

The questions asked throughout this chapter are the kinds of questions the presider might ask in reflecting on the ministry of presiding. Similar questions might be applied to all the dimensions of the presider's ministry listed in chapter two (i.e., leading by example, serving the assembly, knowing the community, planning and preparing the celebration, creating an atmosphere for worship, breaking open the Word, facilitating an experience of church, reflecting a prayerful presence, and building up the kingdom of God).

4. A Spirituality for Liturgical Presiders

After attending a workshop for presiders, Dan wrote the following on his evaluation: "I didn't know there was so much involved in leading prayer. I used to think that it was just a matter of doing and saying the right things. This workshop has helped me to see that presiding is not so much about *doing* as it is about *being a minister* of the church and reflecting God's love to the people who have gathered. Learning the practical details is easy compared to acquiring the attitudes needed to preside effectively. That's the real challenge for me—working to integrate who I am with what I do and say in the liturgy."

By the grace of baptism, all Christians share in the spirit of God's love. Throughout life's journey, the challenge for believers is to enter more deeply into the mystery of God's love, and to allow the grace of God's love to permeate all aspects of life. Spirituality is not something extra added onto life; it is the way one integrates a life of faith with all the other dimensions of one's life.

There are many aspects of a person's spiritual life that are uniquely individual. However, there are some aspects of spirituality that are ecclesial, rooted in one's relationship to God through the church. This is especially true for those who are ministers in the church, for those who exercise an official role of leadership.

Biblical Models

Since all Christian ministry is rooted in the ministry of Jesus, the best model for a spirituality of ministry can be found by looking to him. Scripture and Christian tradition suggest many images that reflect the different dimensions of Jesus' ministry. This chapter will focus on four images from the New Testament that describe Jesus' ministry and that might serve as a starting point for developing a spirituality of presiding.

Servant

The Gospels describe Jesus as servant, as one who came not to be served but to serve others (Mk 10:45). His entire life was in service to the reign of God: proclaiming the good news of salvation, healing the sick, and bringing forgiveness to sinners (Lk 4:16-22). In both word and deed, Jesus worked to empower others to share the fullness of God's life and love (Jn 10:10). Throughout his ministry, Jesus gathered a community of disciples and led them by example to serve others (Jn 13: 1-20). Jesus warned his disciples not to lord their authority over others (Mk 10:42) but to treat others with respect and compassion (Lk 10:25-37). As servant-leader, Jesus challenged his disciples to give their lives in service to the Gospel (Mk 8:31-38). As suffering servant, Jesus gave his own life on the cross (Mt 27: 33-56).

Following the ministry of Jesus, the presider is called to be a servant. The presider serves the community by gathering together the members of the assembly who have come to worship. The presider speaks a gracious word of welcome in the name of Christ, who has called this particular community together. In the name of Christ, the presider both comforts and challenges the community in the proclamation of the Word and in voicing the prayer of the community.

As the one who directs the worship of the community, the presider is called to lead but not to dominate. The presider's role is one of servant-leadership. In this role, the presider recognizes God's presence in the midst of the assembly and empowers the community to assume its rightful role of full, conscious, and active participation in the celebration of the liturgy. Throughout the liturgy, the presider invites the members of the assembly to join their prayer with that of Christ, who offers the sacrifice to the Father.

The presider also serves the assembly by coordinating the planning of the liturgy and by working to ensure the reverent flow of the liturgy. In this regard, the presider directs the other liturgical ministers, recognizes their importance within the celebration, and seeks to coordinate their efforts to serve the worship of the assembly.

Since all of these aspects of serving the community involve working with others for the good of the entire community, the presider must exemplify a basic respect for other ministers and for the members of the assembly. The presider also needs to develop a style of leadership that is strong yet gentle. As the one who both enables and leads the community's worship, the presider's role of servant-leader is a powerful symbol. The presider needs to learn how to use this power effectively and how to share it appropriately with others.

One Who Prays

Throughout the Gospels, especially the Gospel according to Luke, Jesus is portrayed as one who prays. From the time of his baptism (Lk 3:21) until his final hour on the cross (Lk 23:46), prayer was the basis of Jesus' relationship with God and a source of his ministry to others. Jesus prayed when he was alone (Lk 6:12) and in the company of others (Lk 9:16). Jesus prayed with the community as they assembled for Sabbath worship (Lk 4:16), and with the disciples when they gathered to share a meal (Mt 26:26-29). He prayed before feeding the crowd with the loaves and the fish (Mt 14:19), and at table with two disciples who came to know him in the breaking of the bread (Lk 24:30-31). Jesus linked prayer with faith (Mk 11:22-24) and asserted that it is indispensable for casting out certain kinds of demons (Mk 9:29). Jesus taught others to pray (Lk 11:1-4), and described God's response to prayer as a gift of God's Spirit (Lk 11:13).

Just as prayer was the basis for Jesus' relationship with God and a source of strength for his ministry to others, so prayer needs to be an integral part of the life of the presider. The presider needs to grow in a loving relationship with God through prayer. Before the presider can lead others in prayer, a strong personal life of prayer must be cultivated and deepened. This personal prayer enables the presider to develop and manifest a committed and transparent faith while leading the assembly in prayer. As one who prays and leads the assembly in prayer, the presider must acquire the ability to "engage in the liturgical actions and speak the ritual words in such a way that these actions and words will lead the assembly to experience an ever-greater identity with its one Lord as his living Body" (Association of National Secretaries 18).

As one who prays, the presider is called to follow the example of Jesus, whose entire life was characterized by a relationship with God that was shaped by prayer. The presider's personal prayer is the foundation of the ministry of leading the public prayer of the church.

Shepherd

Jesus is also seen as shepherd (Jn 10:11), as one who cares for others with compassion and tenderness (Mt 14:14). Proclaiming the reign of God by word and deed, Jesus responded to others with love and taught others to do the same (Jn 13:34). He showed a special love for those who were poor, marginalized, or alienated (Lk 5:30). Jesus brought healing to the sick (Lk 5:40) and forgiveness to sinners (Lk 7:48). Jesus taught his disciples to forgive not only seven times, but seventy times seven (Mt 19:21-22). He taught them that love of God involves the love of neighbor (Mk 12: 28-31), and he expanded the concept of neighbor to include even those who are one's enemies (Mt 5: 44-45).

The image of the presider as shepherd is rooted in the presider's relationship with the community. It should be a relationship of mutual trust, flowing from the presider's involvement in and care for the community.[1] This day-to-day interaction enables the presider to know the community so as to respond to its needs in a spirit of compassion. As one who walks with the community and who is sensitive to its needs and issues, the presider enables the community to experience the care of Jesus, the good shepherd. By caring for the community and by fostering the care of members for one another, the presider strengthens the bonds of trust and compassion within the community. As one who shepherds the community by sensitivity to its cares and concerns, the presider is able to function more effectively in liturgical ministry to the assembly.

As shepherd, the presider follows the example of Jesus, who nurtures the life of God's Spirit within the community by feeding them with the bread of God's Word and the bread of the Eucharist. By walking with the community and responding to its needs with a pastoral heart, the presider comes to know the physical, spiritual, and emotional hungers of the community. As shepherd of the people of God, the presider must work to facilitate the community's response to those who are in need, so that both its worship and its daily life are faithful to the Gospel of Jesus.

Prophet

A final image to be considered in describing the ministry of Jesus is that of prophet. The Gospels reveal Jesus' life as a prophetic witness to the reign of God (Lk 7:16). Jesus announced that he had come to bring liberty to captives and freedom to those who were oppressed (Lk 4: 18-21). Throughout his ministry, Jesus challenged the institutional structures that oppressed and alienated people (Mt 23:1-36). He confronted evil in its many manifestations and renewed a spirit of hope in the lives of many (Lk 6:17-26). As Jesus instructed his disciples,

---

1 For a fuller discussion of the theological and psychological dimensions of Christian shepherding, see Hiltner. Hiltner notes that "shepherding is our most ancient metaphor for the tender and solicitous concern that the Church and its ministers exercise to all persons in need. The actual work of shepherding has been known more often as pastoral care" (7).

he challenged them to confront evil (Mk 3:14) and to bring God's life to others (Mt 10:1).

Following the example of Jesus, the presider seeks to be a prophetic voice within the community. The presider seeks to proclaim a healing word that will transform the community and enable it to faithfully fulfill its mission of witnessing to the reign of God in the world.

Describing the prophetic dimension of ministry, Walter Brueggemann notes that it "consists of offering an alternative perception of reality and letting people see their own history in the light of God's freedom and his will for justice" (110). He goes on to suggest several characteristics of the prophetic witness. The prophet must be able to criticize what is oppressive, manipulative, and unjust while at the same time enabling, empowering, and energizing people to rise above their human and spiritual plight. The prophet is also called to question the underlying assumptions and the strategic values of the status quo, in order to propose better ways of witnessing to the reign of God. The prophetic outreach is one of sensitivity and imagination. It connects readily with pain, hardship, and suffering, and invites people to commit themselves to the pursuit of justice, peace, and compassion. The prophet also invites people to engage in history. The prophetic dimension of ministry invites people to remember the past and to dream of the future as they seek to find meaning in the present. The prophetic vision allows people to struggle with the ambiguities and tensions in life, and does not seek to propose quick solutions to problems that arise. At the same time, the prophet is called to foster hope as people engage in the contradictions of life, calling them to perseverance in the midst of struggle (109-113).

This description of the prophetic dimension of the minister's role is an apt way to describe the presider's role of fostering the community's transformation into an effective witness of the reign of God. As a prophetic voice, the presider helps the community examine its life in light of the Gospel message. While distinguishing between what the community wants to hear and what the community needs to hear, the presider speaks a message of hope that is both encouraging and challenging. As the one who normally preaches the homily or offers a reflection on the Word of God, the presider fulfills this prophetic dimension by applying the Gospel message to the contemporary life of the community.

In a similar way, the prophetic role of the presider can foster the community's commitment to justice and peace. By naming the injustices both within and beyond the community, the presider seeks to inspire and motivate its members to pursue the demands of justice as they seek to live out their vocation as a sign of God's reign in the world. But this inspiration cannot be limited to the presider's words. The presider's preaching must be affirmed by the witness of a personal commitment to justice. This is reflected in the presider's style of leadership, sense of hospitality and inclusivity, presence to others in the midst of life's struggles, and involvement in the pursuit of justice and peace.

As prophet, the presider seeks to follow the model of Jesus whose life and death were a prophetic witness to the reign of God. By both word and deed, the presider needs to foster the transformation of the community into a living sign of God's presence. When the liturgy and sacraments are celebrated in faith, they transform human experience. The presider's personal faith commitment, as it is expressed in the prophetic dimension of this ministry, seeks to foster and aid that transformation.

Spiritual Attitudes for Presiders

Reflecting on the ministry of the presider as servant, as one who prays, as shepherd and as prophet, suggests a number of attitudes that need to be incorporated into the presider's spirituality. Three will be addressed here: reverence, hospitality, and authenticity. It is important to emphasize that these attitudes and skills are not limited to the presider. Rather, they are attitudes the presider needs to acquire and to foster in others who are called to ministry.

Reverence

Peter Fink describes reverence as "a relational stance of deep respect before a person, or by extension, any reality that is held to be sacred or worthy of honor" (1098). Within the liturgy, the presider needs to cultivate an attitude of reverence for God, reverence for the assembly, reverence for the presider's own ministry, and reverence for the liturgical rites, prayers, symbolic acts, and holy objects.

Within the liturgy, the assembly gathers in the presence of God to listen to God's voice and to raise its own voice in prayer. Reverence for God acknowledges the sacredness of this event as a meeting of God with God's people, and enables one to approach this holy encounter with a sense of wonder and awe. Reverence for God acknowledges the mystery of this sacred moment and seeks to respond in praise of the One who is present in the midst of the people.

Since the assembly itself is a sign of Christ's presence in the liturgy, the presider needs to cultivate an attitude of reverence for the assembly. In both word and gesture, the presider needs to acknowledge the presence of Christ in the gathered community. In the words of greeting, in the dialogues with the assembly, in physical gestures and facial expressions, the presider needs to express a profound respect for the presence of Christ in the assembly.

The presider is another of the signs of Christ's presence within the liturgical assembly. This implies that the words and actions of the presider are the words and actions of Christ. As such, the presider's words and actions must be worthy of the one represented. Following the example of Christ who humbled himself to serve others, the presider needs to see the ministry as a service for others. This humble respect for the presider's own ministry enables the presider to acknowledge with reverence the God who is praised in the midst of the assembly.

Within the liturgy, the presider also needs to manifest a sense of respect for the liturgical rites, prayers, actions, and objects. Nothing is trivial. Rather, all the rites and prayers are sacred, and all the actions and objects are sacramental, because they help to reveal the presence of God. The presider needs to approach the prayers and actions of the liturgical rites and to handle the books, vessels, and other liturgical objects with a sense of reverence and respect.

But the presider's sense of reverence cannot be limited to moments of the liturgy. Jesus' words that what is done to others is done to him (Mt 25:40) suggest that reverence for others is needed in all relationships, both within and outside the moments of liturgical celebration. Recognizing that Christ is present in others, and acknowledging that the presider's own ministry is modeled on the ministry of Jesus who responded to others with love and compassion, the presider needs to manifest an attitude of reverence in all aspects of ministry.

Throughout the presider's ministry as servant, as one who prays, as shepherd, and as prophet, the presider needs to manifest a sense of reverence for God, for others, for the presider's own ministry, and for the rituals and objects of the liturgy. This attitude of reverence is marked by a sense of respect for others and a sense of care for the way in which the presider exercises this ministry.

Hospitality

The *New Dictionary of Sacramental Worship* defines hospitality as "the art or practice of being hospitable; the reception and entertainment of guests, visitors or strangers, with liberality and good will" (Malarcher 562). Within the liturgy, the presider needs to cultivate and foster an attitude of hospitality that helps all who gather feel that they are welcome and included within the celebration. Hospitality flows from a sense of reverence for others. By respecting others and seeing in them the presence of Christ, the presider works to foster a climate of hospitality where all feel that they belong.

Henri Nouwen, a noted spiritual writer, suggests that hospitality implies a sense of gracious welcome, the "creation of a space where the stranger can enter and become a friend instead of an enemy" (8). Nouwen continues:

> A real community has members with different characters,
> different moods, different histories, and different lifestyles. The

> power and beauty of Christian liturgy is that it brings men [and
> women] together in a common awareness of gratitude to God
> by creating a space in which individual differences are not
> denied but respected, and in which many can feel at home (24).

Within the liturgy, the presider's words and actions should help the community to feel at ease, so that they might be comfortable in assuming their rightful place as participants in the liturgy. The presider's role of overseeing the worship of the community further implies that the presider fosters an attitude of hospitality in the other liturgical ministers.

The presider also needs to work at creating an atmosphere and space for the liturgy that is hospitable. The presider needs to be certain that the worship space and the arrangement of furnishings reflect a sense of welcome. In a similar way, decorations should enhance the worship space and help to create a sense of belonging. The presider needs to be attentive to the fact that the altar should only be used to hold the bread and cup and the ritual text and should never be used as a resting place for eyeglasses, notes, or other objects. In a similar way, the presider needs to be certain that the sanctuary remains uncluttered and that unnecessary furnishings are removed. The presider is also responsible to see that the choices of prayers, ritual actions, vesture, and vessels are appropriate to the celebration, and that these choices help the members of the community feel comfortable within the celebration.

The presider must also be conscious of the fact that it is Christ who extends the invitation to the table. Since the presider is often considered as one who ministers *in persona Christi* by gathering the community and voicing its prayer, the presider needs to exemplify the graciousness of Christ in all that is said and done. The presider needs to be certain that all are made to feel welcome, especially those who might feel alienated from the community. In this regard, the presider also needs to impress upon the members of the assembly their important role in the ministry of hospitality.

Throughout the presider's ministry, the presider needs to manifest an attitude of hospitality. This sense is characterized by a gracious welcome to all who gather and an attentiveness to see that all are included within the celebration of the liturgy.

Authenticity

Authenticity is defined as "the quality or state of being authentic, genuine, true" (*Webster's Dictionary*, s.v. "authentic"). For the presider to be authentic means that the presider is a person of integrity and sincerity, that all of the presider's words and actions ring true. Authenticity demands that the presider be conscious of the meaning of the liturgy and seek to be faithful to it in the presider's own life. To be authentic implies "that every word spoken, every gesture performed, every action carried out correspond to the reality which underlies it" (Swayne 56). The presider also needs to be attentive to the authenticity of the signs and symbols used in the liturgy. *Environment and Art in Catholic Worship* (EACW) notes that:

> Every word, gesture, movement, object, appointment must be real in the sense that it is our own. It must come from the deepest understanding of ourselves (not careless, phony, counterfeit, pretentious, exaggerated, etc.). Liturgy has suffered historically from a kind of minimalism and an overriding concern for efficiency, partly because sacramental causality and efficacy have been emphasized at the expense of sacramental signification. As our symbols tended in practice to shrivel up and petrify, they became much more manageable and efficient. They still "caused," were still "efficacious" even though they had often ceased to signify in the richest, fullest sense (14).

> Renewal requires the opening up of our symbols, especially the fundamental ones of bread and wine, water, oil, the laying on of hands, until we can experience all of them as authentic and appreciate their symbolic value (15).

Within the liturgy, the presider needs to be authentic in all words and actions while opening up the meaning of the symbols for the community. The presider must understand and believe in the primacy of the assembly as a liturgical symbol, and understand the presider's own ministry as one of service within the assembly.

In voicing the prayer of the community, the presider also needs to strive for authenticity and to pray from the heart. The presider should be comfortable with prayer, both as one who prays personally and as one who is called to lead the public prayer of the community. The presider needs to be at peace in praying and relaxed while giving voice to the prayer of the people. The presider is to be familiar with the liturgical prayers themselves, praying with them in preparation for the ministry of leading the prayer of the assembly. The presider is also to be familiar and comfortable with the many languages of prayer, so that, when voicing prayer, when leading silence, and when using gesture, the presider is at ease.

As the presider works to develop a presidential style that is authentic, the presider needs to invest the entire self. Hovda notes:

> Part of one's service to the assembly as presider is to be willing to present oneself to the whole group, consenting to be a focal point in the action, being in constant communication with the other ministers and the entire assembly through eye contact, gesture, body posture and movement, as well as word. The self-centered person, the ecclesiastical prince, the person who is out for privileges and status is opaque in this role. If, however, the presider is close to and part of the lives of all in the faith community, one of the people, clearly the servant of all, then there is the possibility of being transparent to the presence and action of the Lord. But it is a transparency that is accomplished, not with an anonymous persona, but with oneself.
>
> So, when one functions as presider or other minister, it is the whole person, the real person, the true person, the full and complete person who functions (*Strong, Loving and Wise* 57).

To be authentic in this role, the presider must understand that, as a focal point in the liturgical action, the presider's role is not to draw attention to the presider but to focus attention on Christ, who leads the assembly in offering its worship to God.

The presider also has a responsibility to see that the liturgy is the authentic prayer of the people. This means fostering their full, active, and conscious participation as well as adapting the liturgy where appropriate to the needs and cultural context of the gathered community.[2] This also implies that the presider is familiar with the ritual nature of the liturgy, as well as its rhythm and flow, so that any adaptations that the presider makes do not trivialize the liturgy.

The presider also needs to assure that what happens in the liturgical celebration is an authentic reflection of the daily life of the community. Here, the presider needs to foster among the members of the community an ongoing sense of mutual care for the needs of one another. The presider needs to encourage the members of the community to become what they receive: the Body of Christ.[3]

Throughout the presider's ministry, in all its dimensions as servant, as one who prays, as shepherd and as prophet, the presider needs to manifest an attitude of authenticity. This implies that the presider's words and actions are genuine and ring true in the minds and hearts of the assembly. All that is done in the liturgy has to spring from the heart and from a genuine love for God and for God's people. This suggests a sense of care and attention to detail in the preparation and celebration of the liturgy, as well as a deep commitment to the understanding of liturgy as the source and summit of the presider's and the community's life of faith.

---

2 For a discussion of the adaptation of the liturgy to various cultures and traditions, see Chupungco, *Liturgies of the Future*, and his earlier work, *Cultural Adaptation of the Liturgy*. See also Weems, who addresses both the need for a pastoral understanding of culture, and the leader's role in attending to the cultural context of a particular community.

3 In one of the homilies to the newly baptized, Augustine reminds them that they are the Body of Christ, and he challenges them to be what they see, and receive what they are. *"Vos autem estis corpus Christi et membra...Estote quod videtis, et accipite quod estis"* (cols. 1247-1248).

PART TWO

Presiding at Specific Liturgical Celebrations

When Claudia asked Brenda to lead the monthly celebration of the Liturgy of the Word with children, Brenda protested: "What qualifications do I have to lead the liturgy? I'm not ordained. I don't know what to do!" Claudia responded, "Who better to lead the children in prayer? You are a mother of four, a great storyteller and a woman of deep faith. And besides that, the kids love you. You can learn the practical details. Fr. John and I will lead you through the process."

Whether leading Liturgy of the Word with children or presiding at Sunday Eucharist, whether presiding at a funeral liturgy or leading Sunday celebrations in the absence of a priest, the presider must learn a number of practical details. The following chapters will describe the presider's role in each of these liturgies.

5. Sunday Eucharist

Throughout the ages, Christians have come together to celebrate their faith. In the domestic churches of the early Christians, in the imperial basilicas of the Roman Empire, in the great cathedrals of the Middle Ages, and in the parish churches of today, Christians have gathered to proclaim the death and resurrection of the Lord in Word and sacrament. In the assembly of believers, in the proclamation of the Word, and in the breaking of the bread, the community celebrates the presence of the risen Lord.

Both *Constitution on the Sacred Liturgy* (CSL) and *General Instruction on the Roman Missal* (GIRM) view the Sunday Eucharist as the church's most fundamental work. It is at Sunday Eucharist that the church finds its true meaning and is strengthened for its mission. Here the church celebrates both the source and summit of its faith. This is true on both the theoretical and practical level, for Sunday is obviously the time when the vast majority of church-going Catholics assemble. In fact, in many parishes, Sunday is most likely the only time that many Catholics come into formal contact with the church as church. For this reason, the Sunday Eucharist needs to be a high priority in the life of the community. This demands a commitment of time, energy, and resources to assure that the Sunday Eucharist is and remains the focal point of the community. For it is here that the community comes to celebrate its life of faith; it is here where the church is renewed to continue its mission.

As noted in *Music in Catholic Worship* (MCW), good celebrations of the liturgy foster and nourish faith, poor celebrations weaken and destroy it. For this reason, every effort must be placed into making Sunday Eucharist a celebration of good quality.

A discussion of quality needs to look beyond the externals of liturgical celebration, since quality is more a function of the interior disposition of the worshiping community, than the result of externals. The interior vitality of faith and love, constantly renewed through the celebration of the liturgy, results in the ongoing conversation mandated by baptism. To the degree that the assembly and its ministers surrender themselves to the Lord in this process of conversion, the liturgy will grow in quality.

In the liturgy, the love of the Lord Jesus enlivens, restores and sends the community forth to renew the face of the earth by sharing the good news of God's love. The quality of the liturgy reflects the degree to which the community has entered into this process of conversion and evangelization.

While there are many criteria that might be used in describing a liturgy of good quality, a liturgy that leads to ongoing conversion in Christ, the following should be considered basic:

- the full, conscious, and active participation by the faithful

- the thoughtful planning and careful preparation of the liturgy

- the appropriate use of trained liturgical ministers

- the use of liturgical music that is appropriate to the celebration

- careful attention to the primary symbols of the liturgy

- a sense of noble simplicity

- the good use of liturgical space

- a homily that is rooted in Scripture and addressed to the local assembly

An important issue related to the quality of Sunday Eucharist is the number of Masses that are scheduled on weekends. In the early days of the church, the community came together under one roof to celebrate the Eucharist on the Lord's day. In this way, by sharing together the one bread and the one cup, the community was joined together as the one Body of Christ. Only when the ideal of one eucharistic assembly became impractical or impossible as the community grew in size, did it become necessary for the community to divide into smaller assemblies, and thus to multiply Masses on the Lord's day.

Over the centuries, the multiplication of Masses became a growing problem and even an abuse in some places. When permission was granted to allow the Saturday evening Mass, many parishes simply added an extra Mass for convenience, without consideration for the real need of the community or for the sense of unity that is celebrated in the Eucharist.

In general, Masses were added to the weekend schedule to provide more opportunities for people to participate in Sunday Eucharist. In some cases, however, the proliferation of Masses, accompanied by shifts in population and the declining number of clergy, has become detrimental to the quality of the Sunday eucharistic celebration.

At some Masses, for example, only a small congregation scattered throughout the church is in attendance, which hardly communicates the sense that all present are united with Christ and with one another in the eucharistic celebration. At other Masses, there are not enough properly trained ministers available to provide the variety of ministries necessary for the liturgy to be celebrated effectively and with the full participation called for in the renewal of the liturgy. In some instances, clergy are overextended and find that they have to celebrate five or six Masses on the weekend (for example, Saturday morning Mass, a funeral or wedding Mass, Saturday evening Mass, and two or three Masses on Sunday morning).

The quality, dignity, preparation, and active, prayerful participation of the people will necessarily limit the number of times any one parish can effectively celebrate the Eucharist on the Lord's day. The schedule for weekend Masses, therefore, should reflect a commitment to the primacy of the Sunday Eucharist and to its quality celebration. Masses should be arranged so that people are brought together for worship and not isolated at celebrations with only a few in attendance. Neither should people be uncomfortably crowded at liturgies with too many people. Mass schedules should allow enough time for the community to gather, to celebrate, and to leave. Mass schedules should honestly reflect the number of clergy and ministers available to provide for quality celebrations of the Eucharist.

The Structure of Sunday Eucharist

GIRM identifies four elements in the structure of the Mass: introductory rites, Liturgy of the Word, Liturgy of the Eucharist, and concluding rite.

Introductory Rites

The parts preceding the liturgy of the word, namely, the entrance song, greeting, penitential rite, *Kyrie*, *Gloria*, and opening prayer or collect, have the character of a beginning, introduction, and preparation.

The purpose of these rites is that the faithful coming together take on the form of a community and prepare themselves to listen to God's word and celebrate the Eucharist properly (24).

Liturgy of the Word

Readings from Scripture and the chants between the readings form the main part of the liturgy of the word. The homily, profession of faith, and general intercessions or prayer of the faithful expand and complete this part of the Mass. In the readings, explained by the homily, God is speaking to his people, opening up to them the mystery of redemption and salvation, and nourishing their spirit; Christ is present to the faithful through his own word. Through the chants the people make God's word their own and through the profession of faith affirm their adherence to it. Finally, having been fed by this word, they make their petitions in the general intercessions for the needs of the church and for the salvation of the whole world (33).

Liturgy of the Eucharist

At the last supper Christ instituted the sacrifice and paschal meal that make the sacrifice of the cross to be continuously present in the Church, when the priest, representing Christ the Lord, carries out what the Lord did and handed over to his disciples to do in his memory....Accordingly, the Church has planned the celebration of the eucharistic liturgy around the parts corresponding to these words and actions of Christ:

1. In the preparation of the gifts, the bread and the wine with water are brought to the altar, that is, the same elements that Christ used.

2. In the eucharistic prayer thanks is given to God for the whole work of salvation and the gifts of bread and wine become the body and blood of Christ.

3. Through the breaking of the one bread the unity of the faithful is expressed and through communion they receive the Lord's body and blood in the same way the apostles received them from Christ's own hands (48).

Concluding Rite

The concluding rite consists of:

a) the priest's greeting and blessing, which on certain days and occasions is expanded and expressed in the prayer over the people or another more solemn formulary;

b) the dismissal of the assembly which sends each member back to doing good works, while praising and blessing the Lord (57).

The Presider's Role at Sunday Eucharist

Throughout the celebration of the Sunday Eucharist, the presider has a crucial role to play. The presider gathers the community and animates and facilitates the prayer of the assembly. It is the presider who facilitates the proclamation of the Word of God and helps the members of the community to make the connection between God's Word and their own lives. It is the presider who voices the prayer of the community during the eucharistic prayer and who shares the sacraments with the faithful. It is the presider who dismisses the community and sends them forth to share the Good News with others.

In the celebration of the Mass, there are three focal points in the sanctuary from which the presider leads the prayer of the community. The introductory rites and the concluding rite are led from the presidential chair. The focal point for the Liturgy of the Word is the ambo. The altar serves as the focus for the Liturgy of the Eucharist. All three are important primary symbols within the liturgy and should be visible to the entire assembly. Care should be taken not to obscure these primary symbols with decorations. For example, during the Christmas season, the creche should never be placed in front of the altar.

Ideally, the presider's chair should stand alone to highlight the role of the one who is leading the prayer of the assembly. If there is a deacon present, the deacon sits to the presider's right. Servers should not flank the presider, but should sit in a place from which they can assist the presider as necessary. There is no need for servers or the other liturgical ministers to be seated in the sanctuary. They can take their place within the assembly and come forward when it is time for them to minister.

Planning and Preparing for Sunday Mass

Prior to the celebration of the liturgy, there are a number of responsibilities that the presider should assume. This includes both long-term planning and immediate preparation for the liturgy. While there may be a liturgy coordinator in the parish who is responsible for some of these details, it is the presider's ultimate responsibility to be certain that all is in order for the celebration of the liturgy.

Long-term planning of the liturgy includes:

- meeting with the liturgy team to plan the liturgical environment for the seasons;

- meeting with the musicians for the selection of music for the liturgy;

- meeting with a homily preparation group who assist in the preparation of the homily;

- reviewing the scheduling and selection of appropriate liturgical ministers for the celebration;

- coordinating the roles of the other liturgical ministers.

Immediate preparation of the liturgy involves:

- checking to determine that there are an adequate number of ministers to assist in the celebration of the liturgy: cantor, special ministers of the Eucharist, lectors, ministers of hospitality, servers;

- choosing the liturgical texts from among the options in the sacramentary;

- preparing any introductory comments;

- preparing the liturgical books (sacramentary and lectionary);

- preparing the vessels and the bread and wine;

- alerting the cantor to any introductory announcements.

Introductory Rites

In the liturgical assembly of the church, the risen Lord is present. The purpose of the introductory rites is to help the assembly to become aware of its identity as the Body of Christ, to prepare to hear the Word of God, and to celebrate the Eucharist.

The role of the presider during the introductory rites is to extend a gracious welcome to the assembly gathered in the name of Christ, to invite the community to prepare for the celebration, and to voice the prayer of God's people in the opening prayer.

Entrance Song

- During the entrance song, the first element of the introductory rites, the presider goes to the altar in the procession of ministers, makes a deep bow to the altar (in the presence of the tabernacle, the ministers genuflect), kisses the altar, (incenses the altar if incense is used), and goes to the presidential chair.

  The procession of ministers through and from the assembly helps to visibly express the relationship of the presider and the ministers to the gathered community: the presider and the other ministers are part of the assembly. GIRM lists the order of the entrance procession:

  a) a server with lighted censer, if incense is used;

  b) the servers, who according to the occasion, carry lighted candles, and between them the cross-bearer, if the cross is to be carried;

  c) acolytes and other ministers;

  d) a reader who may carry the Book of the Gospels (or the lectionary, if the Book of Gospels is not used);

  e) the priest who is to celebrate Mass.

If a deacon is present, the deacon carries the Book of
Gospels and precedes the presider in the procession.
If the deacon carries the Book of Gospels, the lectionary
should be placed on the ambo before the celebration,
since only one book should be carried in the procession.
The lectionary to be used in the celebration of Liturgy of
the Word with children should also be placed on or near
the ambo before the celebration begins.

Greeting

- After making the sign of the cross, the presider extends a
  formal greeting to the assembly and may then introduce
  the Mass of the day.

- Because Mass begins with the entrance song, it is not
  appropriate for the presider to say, "Let us *begin* our
  celebration in the name of the Father…"

- The greeting of the Mass is meant to be a formal
  exchange between the presider and the assembly who
  mutually acknowledge Christ's presence in their midst
  (for example, "The Lord be with you." "And also with
  you.") For this reason, it is not appropriate to greet the
  assembly with a merely human exchange (for example,
  "Good Morning").

- During the greeting, the presider extends his hands.
  This should be a broad gesture that helps to acknowledge
  God's presence in the midst of the assembly. As the
  people respond to the greeting, the presider closes his
  hands.

- As the presider voices the greeting and gestures with his
  hands, the presider should also make eye contact with
  members of the assembly. The presider should continue

looking at the members of the assembly as they make their response.

- If the presider chooses to introduce the Mass at this point, the presider's comments, which set the tone of the celebration, should be brief and well prepared. At this point, the presider may briefly welcome any guests or special groups who are present. The key here is to keep comments succinct and to the point.

- In introducing the Mass, the presider should be very careful not to impose a theme on the liturgy. The one theme of every liturgy is the paschal mystery of the Lord. While different celebrations may reflect different dimensions of the paschal mystery, all celebrations are meant to lead the members of the assembly deeper into the mystery of Christ's death and resurrection.

- Once the liturgy has begun, it is not appropriate for the presider to invite the members of the assembly to introduce themselves to one another. Members of the assembly should be encouraged to greet one another as they arrive, in preparation for the celebration of the liturgy.

Penitential Rite

- The presider then introduces the penitential rite.

- Three introductions are provided in the sacramentary for the introduction to the penitential rite, but the presider may also introduce the rite using "similar words" to those found in the sacramentary.

- On occasion, it may be appropriate to incorporate the introduction to the penitential rite into the introductory remarks that follow the greeting.

- The presider should use an economy of words, however, and not turn the invitation to the penitential rite into a mini-homily.

- When Form C of the penitential rite is used, the presider should remember that the invocations are not petitions for forgiveness for particular wrongs committed. They are invocations that invite the community to praise God for the salvation revealed in Christ. As such, the invocations are addressed to Christ and not to the Father or the Spirit.

- The rite of blessing and sprinkling with holy water may take the place of the penitential rite. This rite seems to be especially appropriate during the Easter season.

Gloria

- The Gloria is used on the Sundays outside Advent and Lent.

- Ideally, the Gloria, a hymn of praise, is to be sung. If it is not sung, it is recited.

Opening Prayer

- The presider then sings or says the opening prayer that completes the introductory rites.

- The presider makes the invitation to prayer with hands closed, after which all pray in silence for a few moments.

- The presider then extends hands in the "orans" position and sings or says the prayer aloud.

- As the presider makes the Trinitarian conclusion to the prayer, the presider closes the hands to coincide with the end of the prayer.

Liturgy of the Word

The celebration of the Liturgy of the Word includes several elements and several ministers. Ideally, each of the readings is proclaimed by a separate minister. The faithful are called to listen to the Word, reflect on it in silence, respond to it in song, and apply it to their daily lives. Inspired by the Word, the community professes its faith and prays for the needs of the church and the world.

During the Liturgy of the Word, the presider's role is to be attentive to the proclamation of the Word, to preach the homily, to lead the profession of faith, and to introduce and conclude the prayers of the faithful.

Biblical Readings

- The presider sets the example for the assembly by focusing attention on the ambo and on the reader.

- It is not appropriate for the presider to be reading along in a missalette or to be gazing out into the assembly during the proclamation of the Word.

Responsorial Psalm

- After a period of silent reflection on the Word, the presider joins the assembly in singing the responsorial psalm.

Gospel Acclamation

- The Gospel acclamation traditionally accompanies the Gospel procession as the Book of Gospels is carried in procession from the altar to the ambo. If incense is used, it is prepared after the second reading, before the Gospel procession.

- As the Gospel acclamation begins, the presider stands and joins in singing the acclamation. If the acclamation is not sung, it is omitted.

- If a deacon is to read the Gospel, the presider gives a blessing to the deacon.

- If the presider reads the Gospel, the presider bows before the altar and silently recites the prescribed prayer.[1]

Gospel

- The proclamation of the Gospel is not a presidential function. The Gospel is normally proclaimed by a deacon. If no deacon is present, it is proclaimed by a priest other than the one presiding. Only if no deacon or other priest is present is the Gospel read by the priest who presides.

- The Gospel reader greets the people with "The Lord be with you." While greeting the assembly and while the assembly makes its response, it is appropriate for the Gospel reader to look at the assembly.

- While announcing the Gospel passage, the Gospel reader makes the sign of the cross on the book, then on the forehead, lips, and heart.

- At the end of the Gospel, the Gospel reader says, "The Gospel of the Lord," to which the people make their response. It is not appropriate to raise the book high during these words because the "Gospel" is much more than the words in the book. The phrase "The Gospel of the Lord" refers to the word that was spoken, the word that was heard, the word that now takes root in the hearts of the assembly, as well as the words in the book. To

---

1 If a priest other than the presider reads the Gospel, the priest prepares for the Gospel by bowing before the altar and reciting the prescribed prayer. A priest does not request a blessing from another priest who is presiding. If the principal celebrant is a bishop, however, a priest who reads the Gospel does request a blessing from the bishop.

raise the book may serve to draw undue attention
to the printed word.

- Then the Gospel reader kisses the Gospel book and says
  inaudibly, "May the words of the Gospel wipe away
  our sins."

Homily

- The homily is an integral part of the liturgy and should
  not be omitted on Sundays and holy days without a
  serious reason. The homily should be rooted in the
  Scripture and addressed to the particular assembly that
  has gathered.

- The presider may give the homily from the ambo
  or the chair.

Profession of Faith

- The profession of faith serves as a way for the assembly
  to assent to the Word of God as proclaimed in the
  readings. The presider leads the profession of faith that
  all say together.

- The presider leads the community in a gesture
  of reverence (bow) during the words, "By the power
  of the Holy Spirit he was born of the Virgin Mary
  and became man."

Prayers of the Faithful

- The presider introduces the prayers of the faithful by
  inviting the community to intercede for all God's people.

- The introduction is addressed to the people, not to God.

- The intercessions are announced by a deacon, cantor,
  reader, or other minister. The intercessions should
  include prayers: 1) for the church, 2) for public

authorities, 3) for those oppressed by any need, and 4) for the local community. In particular celebrations, the intercessions may refer more specifically to the particular event.

- It is not necessary to remember the faithful departed during the prayers of the faithful. The dead are remembered during the eucharistic prayer at Mass and during the intercessions of Evening Prayer. If the dead are to be remembered during the intercessions, care should be taken to avoid using the words, "for whom this Mass is offered," when referring to a particular intention for the liturgy. Every Mass is offered for all the living and all the dead.

- The presider extends his hands and concludes the prayers of the faithful by asking God to hear the prayers of the people "through Christ our Lord."

- The presider might choose the alternate opening prayer to conclude the prayers of the faithful, or the presider might compose the concluding prayer. The following structure and example is given as a model for this prayer:

STRUCTURE	EXAMPLE
You	God our creator,
who	you always hear the prayer of your people.
do	Open our hearts to receive the answer you give us
through	through Christ our Lord.
	Amen.

Liturgy of the Eucharist

During the Liturgy of the Eucharist, the assembly presents the gifts of bread and wine, gives thanks to God for the whole work of salvation and for the gifts of bread and wine that become the Body and Blood of Christ, and enters into communion with the risen Lord and with one another through the reception of the sacrament.

The presider receives the gifts from members of the community and prepares the gifts at the altar. During the eucharistic prayer, the presider voices the church's great prayer of thanksgiving and invites the community to join their sacrifice to that of Christ who offers it to the Father. In the communion rite, the presider invites the assembly to pray the Lord's prayer, breaks the bread, and shares communion with the faithful.

Preparation of the Altar and Gifts

- This entire part of the liturgy is to be seen as a moment of preparation within the Liturgy of the Eucharist. As such, it is a minor element compared to the eucharistic prayer and the communion rite and should not be overemphasized.

- First the altar is prepared by another minister with the corporal, the purificator, the missal, and the chalice (unless the chalice is prepared at a side table).

- The presider receives the gifts of bread and wine brought forward by members of the assembly.

- The presider may also receive the monetary offering of the community or gifts for the poor. These may be placed near the altar, but never on it.

- The presider takes the bread, and holding it slightly raised above the altar, says the prescribed prayer inaudibly. This gesture is not one of offering or of showing the gifts to the people. The gifts are to be raised *slightly* above the altar, not over one's head. If there is no song at this point, the presider *may* say the words in an audible voice.

- By definition, "inaudible" means "not audible." This means that the prayers are to be said so that they are not heard—in other words, silently. When prayers are said inaudibly, it is not necessary to mouth the words.

- The deacon (or the priest) next pours wine and a little water into the chalice, saying the prescribed words inaudibly. Water is only poured into the chalice. If flagons or other cups are used, water is not poured into them.

- Then the presider takes the chalice, and holding it slightly raised above the altar, says the prescribed prayer inaudibly. If there is no song at this point, the presider *may* say the words in an audible voice.

- The presider bows and says the next prayer inaudibly.

- The presider may incense the gifts and the altar.

- The washing of hands is meant to be a real cleansing. An ample amount of water should be poured over the hands (not just the fingertips), and a real towel should be used to allow this symbol to speak as it should.

- After washing hands and saying the prayer inaudibly, the presider then extends and closes hands, while inviting the assembly to prayer. After the people make their response, the presider again extends hands and prays the prayer over the gifts.

Eucharistic Prayer

- The eucharistic prayer is composed of several elements: thanksgiving (preface), acclamation (Sanctus), epiclesis (invocation of the Spirit), institution narrative and consecration, anamnesis (memorial), offering, intercessions, and final doxology. Through the eucharistic prayer, the entire assembly joins itself to Christ in acknowledging the great things God has done and in offering the sacrifice.

- The presider should choose the eucharistic prayer that is most appropriate for the occasion and for the gathered assembly. Careful planning will ensure that Eucharistic Prayer II is not chosen every week because of its brevity.

Preface Dialogue

- Throughout the preface dialogue, it is appropriate for the presider to make eye contact with members of the assembly.

- The presider extends hands and greets the assembly.

- The presider then raises the arms and invites the assembly to lift up their hearts and to give thanks to the Lord.

Preface

- The presider, with hands extended, prays the prayer of thanksgiving and invites the assembly to join with the angels and saints in the acclamation of praise.

- Since the eucharistic prayer is addressed to God, it is not appropriate for the presider to sustain eye contact with members of the assembly throughout the prayer. On occasion, however, it might be appropriate to look at the assembly; for example, when praying the words "Lord, remember your church throughout the world…" or "Have mercy on us all…."

Acclamation

- The presider joins hands at the end of the preface and sings the Sanctus with the people.

Epiclesis

- The presider continues the eucharistic prayer with hands extended. During the epiclesis, the presider extends hands over the offerings and makes the sign of the cross over the gifts.

Institution Narrative and Consecration

- The presider joins the hands for the institution narrative and takes the bread and cup in hand for the words of consecration.

- After the consecration of the bread, the presider shows the consecrated host to the people, then genuflects. This gesture of showing is distinct from both the gesture of placing the gifts on the altar and the gesture of raising the gifts during the doxology. Here, the presider is simply told to show the consecrated elements to the people. It is not necessary to raise them high at this point.

- After the consecration of the wine, the presider shows the cup to the people, then genuflects.

Anamnesis

- With hands joined, the presider invites the assembly to proclaim the mystery of faith.

- After singing the memorial acclamation with the assembly, the presider extends hands and recalls the death, resurrection, and ascension of the Lord.

Offering

- As the presider continues to voice the prayer of the church with hands extended, the community joins its sacrifice to that of Christ and offers it to the Father.

Intercessions

- Continuing with hands extended, the presider prays for the entire church and its members, living and deceased, who are called to share in the salvation Christ offers by communion in his body and blood.

Final Doxology

- Then the presider takes the bread and cup, lifts them up, and sings the final doxology. This elevation is a gesture that is more significant than the earlier gestures of raising the gifts slightly over the altar or of showing the consecrated elements to the people. It is appropriate to raise the gifts high and allow the gesture, as well as the words of the doxology, to invite the people's great Amen.

- The presider continues to hold the gifts as the people respond with their Amen.

Lord's Prayer

- With hands joined together, the presider invites the assembly to pray the Lord's Prayer.

- The presider extends hands to pray the Lord's Prayer and the embolism.

- The presider joins hands as the people pray the doxology.

Sign of Peace

- The presider extends the hands while praying the prayer for peace. The presider joins hands at the conclusion of the prayer.

- The presider then extends and joins the hands while saying, "The peace of the Lord be with you always."

- The presider then invites the people to exchange the sign of peace. The presider gives the sign of peace to the deacon or to the other ministers.

Breaking of Bread

- While the Lamb of God is sung, the presider breaks the bread while other ministers prepare the cups.

- The presider may be assisted by the deacon or communion ministers in the breaking of the bread.

- After breaking the bread, the presider places a small piece of the consecrated bread in the chalice and says the prescribed prayer inaudibly.

Private Preparation of the Priest

- The private prayer of preparation is said inaudibly by the presider with hands joined.

Communion

- The presider shows a piece of the consecrated bread to the people while saying, "This is the Lamb of God…" When communion is distributed under both kinds, as should normally be the case, it may be appropriate to show both the consecrated bread and the cup to the people.

- The presider continues to hold the consecrated gifts as the people say, "Lord, I am not worthy…"

- Before receiving communion, the presider says inaudibly, "May the body of Christ bring me to everlasting life," and "May the blood of Christ bring me to everlasting life."

- The presider then shares communion with the ministers and the people.

- The vessels are cleaned by the presider, a deacon, or a special minister after communion (preferably at a side table) or after Mass.

Prayer after Communion

- The presider may return to the chair for a period of silence or a song of praise.

- Then the presider stands, and with hands joined, invites all to pray.

- The presider extends hands and sings or says the prayer after communion.

Concluding Rite

Announcements

- If there are any announcements, they are made at this time by the presider, deacon, or another minister.

- Announcements should be brief. It is not appropriate to read the parish bulletin to the assembly.

Greeting

- The presider extends hands while saying, "The Lord be with you."

- The presider continues to look at the people as they make their response.

Blessing

- The presider then gives the blessing, making the sign of the cross over the assembly while praying the words, "May almighty God bless you: the Father, the Son, and the Holy Spirit."

- It is not appropriate for the priest to say, "May almighty God bless us..." or to bless himself. The presider's role of leadership means that the presider makes the sign of the cross over the people while saying, "May almighty God bless you..."

- On certain occasions, the presider may use the solemn form of the blessing or the prayer over the people.

Dismissal

- The deacon (or the presider) dismisses the people, sending them forth to do good works and to praise and bless the Lord.

- The presider kisses the altar as at the beginning, bows with the ministers, and leaves.

6. Sunday Celebrations in the Absence of a Priest

Because the celebration of the Sunday Eucharist is at the heart of the life of the church, any discussion of Sunday celebrations in the absence of a priest must emphasize the fact that these celebrations are to be seen as exceptions to the norm. It is only when there is no reasonable opportunity to provide for the celebration of the Mass that "local bishops may judge it necessary to provide for other Sunday celebrations in the absence of a priest, so that in the best way possible, the weekly gathering of the faithful can be continued and the Christian tradition regarding Sunday be preserved. (See *Directory*, no. 6.)" (SCAP 8).

Both the *Directory for Sunday Celebrations in the Absence of a Priest* (DSCAP) and *Sunday Celebrations in the Absence of a Priest: Leader's Edition* (SCAP) make it clear that certain conditions must be met before it is permissible to hold Sunday celebrations in the absence of a priest. When these conditions are met, and the bishop has authorized Sunday celebrations in the absence of a priest, the celebration may take the form of either Liturgy of the Hours or Liturgy of the Word. In both of these cases, the community celebrates the presence of the risen Lord in the liturgical assembly and in the proclamation of the Word. In both instances, the ritual text also makes a provision for the sharing of holy communion.

The distinction between Mass and Sunday celebrations in the absence of a priest, however, must be understood clearly by the community. Nothing that is proper to the Mass, especially the presentation of gifts and the eucharistic prayer, is to be inserted into the celebration. (This implies that when Mass is celebrated, those elements that are distinctive to the Mass—e.g., eucharistic prayer, breaking the bread, and communion under both kinds—must be full and clear.) Proper catechesis of the faithful and proper formation for the presider and other liturgical ministers are essential.

The Structure of Sunday Celebrations in the Absence of a Priest

The first form for Sunday celebrations in the absence of a priest is that of Morning or Evening Prayer from the Liturgy of the Hours. The basic structure of the rite is outlined below.

- **Introductory Rites:** The purpose of these rites serves to gather the faithful into a worshiping community.

- **Psalmody:** Psalms and canticles give the faithful the opportunity to offer praise and thanksgiving to God.

- **Liturgy of the Word:** Through the proclamation of the Word, God speaks to the assembly. By both the Gospel canticle and the intercessions, the community responds to God's Word in thanksgiving and petition.

- **[Communion Rite]:** Though the assembly does not celebrate the Eucharist, provision is made for the sharing of holy communion; the assembly thereby unites itself to the paschal mystery of Christ and to the faithful who are able to celebrate the Eucharist on that particular day.

- **Concluding Rite:** This rite serves to send the assembly forth with God's blessing to live the Christian life. The texts provided in the ritual text for Morning and Evening Prayer are given as a common form and by way of example. The texts proper to each Sunday contained in the Liturgy of the Hours may always be used. Music is an essential part of the rite and should always be part of each celebration.

The second form for the Sunday celebrations in the absence of a priest is that of the Liturgy of the Word. It consists of the following elements:

- **Introductory Rites**

- **Liturgy of the Word**

- **Thanksgiving:** After the Liturgy of the Word, the faithful are invited to praise the glory and mercy of God. This is done by use of a psalm, canticle, hymn litany of praise, or a prayer.

- **Communion Rite**

- **Concluding Rite**

The Presider's Role at Sunday Celebrations in the Absence of a Priest

Either a deacon or a layperson appointed by the bishop may lead Sunday celebrations in the absence of a priest. The roles of each are clearly defined in the Introduction to SCAP.[1]

Deacons (SCAP 18-20)

As a minister of the Word, who also has a responsibility for the sacraments, the deacon is called in a special way to lead these Sunday assemblies. Since the deacon has been ordained for the nurture and increase of the people of God, it belongs to him to lead the prayers, to proclaim the gospel, to preach the homily, and to give communion. (See *Directory*, no. 29; see Paul VI, Motu propro *Ad Pascendum* [15 August 1972], no. 1.).

---

1 SCAP uses the word "preside" to describe the deacon's role at Sunday celebrations in the absence of a priest, and notes that the deacon is to use the presidential chair. When referring to a layperson, SCAP uses the word "lead," and notes that the layperson is to use a chair distinct from the presidential chair.

When a deacon presides at a Sunday celebration in the absence of a priest, he acts in the usual manner in regard to the greetings, the prayers, the gospel reading and homily, the giving of communion, and the dismissal and blessing. He wears the vestments proper to his ministry, that is, the alb with stole, and, as circumstances suggest, the dalmatic. He uses the presidential chair. (See *Directory*, no. 38).

The deacon is always to be assisted by other ministers who will proclaim the Scriptures, assist him in the distribution of holy communion, sing the psalms and other songs, provide instrumental music, and prepare the place for the celebration. (See *Directory*, no. 40).

Laypersons (SCAP 21-24)

In the absence of both a priest and a deacon, upon the request and recommendation of the pastor, the bishop is to appoint persons, lay or religious, who are to be entrusted with the care of leading these celebrations, namely, with leading the prayers, with the ministry of the word, and, when it is to be included in the celebration, with giving holy communion.

These ministers carry out their responsibilities in virtue of their baptism and confirmation. (See *Codex Iuris Canonici* 1983 [hereafter, *CIC*], can. 1248, §2.) Such persons are to be chosen in view of the consistency of their way of life with the Gospel and in the expectation of their being acceptable to the community of the faithful. The appointment of such ministers is made by the bishop for a definite time. Their appointment is to be made known to the community by means of a liturgical celebration in which prayers are offered to God on behalf of those appointed. The Order for the Blessing of Those Who Exercise Pastoral Service (see The Roman Ritual, *Book of Blessings*, Part VI, Chapter 60)...may be used for this purpose.

The pastor is to see to the suitable and continuous instruction of these laypersons and to assist them in the preparation of worthy celebrations. (See *Directory*, no. 30).

The laypersons appointed as leaders should regard the office entrusted to them not so much as an honor but as a responsibility and, above all, as a service to their brothers and sisters under the authority of the pastor. (See *Directory*, no. 27; see *CIC*, can. 230, §3). They "should do all of, but only, those parts which pertain to that office." (See Vatican Council II, Constitution on the Liturgy *Sacrosanctum Concilium* [hereafter *SC*], art. 28.) They should carry out their office with sincere devotion and with the decorum demanded by such a responsibility and rightly expected of them by God's people. (See *Directory*, no 31; see *SC*, art. 29.)

The leader who is a layperson uses the special forms indicated in the rites for the greeting and blessing, does not use words that are proper to a priest or deacon, and omits those rites, gestures, and texts that are too readily associated with the Mass and which might give the impression that the layperson is a sacred minister. (See *Directory*, no. 39; see *General Instruction of the Liturgy of the Hours* [hereafter *GILH*], no. 258; see also the Roman Ritual, *Book of Blessings*, nos. 48, 119, 130, 181.)

The layperson wears vesture that is suitable for his or her function or the vesture prescribed by the bishop. (See The Roman Ritual, *Holy Communion and Worship of the Eucharist outside Mass*, no. 20.) A layperson does not use the presidential chair. ("He or she does not use the presidential chair, but another chair prepared outside the sanctuary" [*Directory*, no. 40]. See also *GILH*, no. 258.) Since the altar is the table of sacrifice and of the paschal banquet, its only use in one of these celebrations is for the rite of communion, when the eucharist is placed on it at the beginning of the communion rite.

The leader is always to be assisted by other ministers who will proclaim the Scriptures, assist in the distribution of holy communion, sing the psalms and other songs, provide instrumental music, and prepare the place for the celebration. (See *Directory*, no. 40.)

Planning and Preparing for Sunday Celebrations in the Absence of a Priest

Prior to the celebration of the liturgy, there are a number of responsibilities that the presider should assume. This includes both long-term planning and immediate preparation for the liturgy. While there may be a liturgy coordinator in the parish who is responsible for some of these details, it is the presider's ultimate responsibility to be certain that all is in order for the celebration of the liturgy.

Long-term planning for Sunday celebrations in the absence of a priest includes:

- studying the ritual structure and liturgical texts for SCAP;

- meeting with the pastor and/or pastoral administrator to determine which form of the liturgy—Liturgy of the Hours (with holy communion) or Liturgy of the Word (with holy communion)—best fits the needs of this community;

- meeting with the musicians to integrate the function of music within the liturgy.

Immediate preparation of the liturgy involves:

- checking to determine that there are an adequate number of ministers to assist in the celebration of the liturgy: cantor, communion ministers (when holy communion is to be shared), lectors, ministers of hospitality;

- preparing the liturgical books (SCAP and lectionary);

- choosing the liturgical texts from among the options in the ritual book;

- turning off the tabernacle alarm and placing the tabernacle key next to the tabernacle (when holy communion is to be shared);

- if the presider is not a deacon, preparing a separate chair (distinct from the presidential chair).

Gestures

- The rubrics of SCAP make no reference to the leader extending hands during the prayers. Perhaps this is because it is assumed that the presider would be holding the ritual book and would not be able to extend hands in prayer.

- If there is a server present to assist the leader by holding the book, it might be appropriate for the leader to extend hands when praying the opening prayer, the Lord's Prayer, and the prayer after communion.

Form I of Sunday Celebrations in the Absence of a Priest: Morning and Evening Prayer (with Holy Communion)

Introductory Rites

- When the assembly has gathered, all stand while the leader, making the sign of cross, sings or says the invitatory: "God come to my assistance." After the people make their response, including the doxology (Glory be), a suitable hymn is sung.

- There is no explicit provision for an entrance procession of ministers.

- Depending on the circumstances, it might be appropriate for the ministers to enter in procession through the midst of the assembly. On other occasions, the ministers might simply take their places before the liturgy begins.

- When a deacon presides, the deacon leads the introductory rites from the presidential chair. When a layperson presides, a chair distinct from the presidential chair is used.

- In the introduction at the beginning of the celebration (or at some other point), the leader should inform the assembly where the pastor is celebrating the Eucharist on that particular Sunday and urge the assembly to unite itself in spirit with that community.

- This announcement might take place before the presider invites the assembly to stand for the introductory rites. (For example, the presider might say: "Brothers and sisters, we gather today as God's holy people. Our pastor, Fr. Lance, is celebrating Eucharist today at Holy Rosary Church, where they also pray for us. As we worship, we join our hearts and voices with all God's people who gather this day to hear God's Word and to share God's love." The presider then gestures for the assembly to stand. The presider then makes the sign of the cross while reciting the invitatory.)

- This announcement might also be made after the invitatory, before the hymn. (For example, the presider might say: "Brothers and sisters, as we gather in prayer today, our pastor is unable to be with us. He is celebrating Eucharist at Holy Rosary Church. One with all our sisters and brothers who are united in prayer this day, let us raise our voices in praise as we sing...."

Psalmody

- At Morning Prayer, the psalmody takes the form of psalm, canticle, psalm. At Evening Prayer, the psalmody takes the form of psalm, psalm, canticle. Before each of the psalms and the canticle, the proper antiphon is sung by the cantor, choir, or entire assembly. The antiphon may be repeated by all at the end of the psalm or after each strophe, as is usually done with the Responsorial Psalm at Mass. All may be seated during the psalmody.

- If the psalms are recited, the leader recites the proper antiphon and then invites the assembly to join in reciting the psalm antiphonally (side to side) or all together.

- At the conclusion of the psalms, the presider may stand and pray the psalm prayer, after which the proper antiphon may be repeated.

- There is no prayer at the end of the canticles.

Liturgy of the Word

- The Liturgy of the Word takes place as at Mass. The readings are those assigned in the *Lectionary for Mass* for that particular Sunday.

Biblical Readings

- During the readings, the presider attends to the proclamation of the word.

- The presider sets the example for the assembly by focusing attention on the ambo and on the reader.

- It is not appropriate for the presider to be reading along in a missalette or to be gazing out into the assembly during the proclamation of the Word.

Responsorial Psalm

- After a period of silent reflection on the Word, the presider joins the assembly in singing the responsorial psalm.

Gospel Acclamation

- The Gospel acclamation is sung before the proclamation of the Gospel. During the Gospel acclamation, the presider moves to the ambo.

Gospel

- A deacon proclaims the Gospel in the usual manner. A layperson omits the greeting, "The Lord be with you," before reading the Gospel.

- While announcing the Gospel passage, the Gospel reader makes the sign of the cross on the book, then on the forehead, lips, and breast.

- At the end, the Gospel reader adds, "The Gospel of the Lord," to which the people make their response. After saying, "The Gospel of the Lord," the Gospel reader should wait until the people make their response, "Praise to you, Lord Jesus Christ," before kissing the book.

- Then the Gospel reader kisses the Gospel book and says inaudibly, "May the words of the Gospel wipe away our sins."

Homily

- A presider who is a deacon gives a homily. When the presider is a layperson who has not been delegated to preach, the pastor may prepare a homily to be read during the celebration. In other cases, when a layperson has been delegated to preach by the bishop, he or she may give those present a brief explanation of the biblical text, so that they may understand through faith the meaning of the celebration. After the homily, there may be a period of silence for reflection on the Word of God.

- After the homily, the deacon returns to the presidential chair, the layperson to his or her chair.

Response to the Word of God

- As a response to God's Word, a responsorial chant or short responsory may be sung. The text of SCAP offers several options.

- This element of the rite is part of the usual pattern of the Liturgy of the Hours, and follows the proclamation of a single passage from Scripture. When three readings are proclaimed, with the accompanying responsorial psalm and Gospel acclamation, it may be preferable to omit this response.

Dismissal of the Catechumens

- If holy communion is to be shared, and there are catechumens present, SCAP provides several options for their dismissal.

Gospel Canticle

- At Morning Prayer, all stand and sing the Canticle of Zachariah. At Evening Prayer, all stand and sing Mary's Canticle. The proper antiphon to the day may be sung before the canticle. It may be repeated at the end of each strophe or at the end of the canticle.

Intercessions

- The presider introduces the intercessions, then another minister sings or recites the intentions.

- If holy communion is not to be shared, the intercessions are concluded with the Lord's Prayer, the concluding prayer, and the concluding rite.

- If holy communion is to be shared, the communion rite follows immediately.

Communion Rite

- The presider then goes to the tabernacle, takes the vessel containing the consecrated bread, places it on the altar, and genuflects.

Lord's Prayer/Sign of Peace

- A presider who is a layperson returns to his or her chair and introduces the Lord's Prayer and the sign of peace. After the sign of peace the layperson returns to the altar for the invitation to communion. A presider who is a deacon remains at the altar for the Lord's Prayer and the Sign of Peace.

Invitation to Communion

- The presider genuflects, takes the host, shows it to the people, and recites the invitation to communion.

Communion

- The presider then receives communion and is assisted by others, if necessary, in sharing communion with members of the assembly. After communion, if any consecrated bread remains, it is placed in the tabernacle. A period of silence may be observed, or a song of praise may be sung.

Prayer after Communion

- The presider then returns to the chair and prays the prayer after communion.

Concluding Rite

- The concluding rite includes the announcements, the collection of the monetary offerings of the assembly, the blessing, and dismissal.

- Announcements concerning parish life and activities may be made, but they should be kept brief.

- A presider who is a deacon says, "The Lord be with you," and then blesses the people.

- A presider who is not a deacon makes the sign of the cross on himself or herself while saying, "May the Lord bless us, protect us from evil, and bring us to everlasting life."

- The presider then dismisses the people.

- If there was an entrance procession of the ministers, it would be appropriate for the ministers to leave in procession.

Form II of Sunday Celebrations in the Absence of a Priest: Liturgy of the Word (with Holy Communion)

Introductory Rites

- When the assembly has gathered, a suitable song may be sung. After singing, all make the sign of the cross.

- There is no explicit provision for an entrance procession of ministers.

- Depending on the circumstances, it might be appropriate for the ministers to enter in procession through the midst of the assembly. On other occasions, the ministers might simply take their places before the liturgy begins.

- A deacon leads the introductory rites from the presidential chair. A layperson leads the introductory rites from a chair distinct from the presidential chair.

Greeting

- The presider greets the people using one of the formulae found in SCAP. There are separate greetings for use by a deacon and a layperson.

Introduction

- In the introduction at the beginning of the celebration, the presider should inform the assembly where the pastor is celebrating the Eucharist on that particular Sunday and urge the assembly to unite itself in spirit with that community. A sample text is provided in SCAP.

Litany in Praise of God's Mercy

- After the presider invites the community to proclaim God's mercy, the leader or another minister (cantor) makes the invocations.

- Unlike the penitential rite at Mass, the litany in praise of God's mercy does not conclude with the absolution, "May almighty God...."

The Opening Prayer

- The presider invites all to pray. After a period of silence, the presider says the prayer of the day.

Liturgy of the Word

- The Liturgy of the Word takes place as at Mass. The readings are those assigned in the *Lectionary for Mass* for that particular Sunday

Biblical Readings

- During the readings, the presider attends to the proclamation of the Word.

- The presider sets the example for the assembly by focusing attention on the ambo and on the reader.

- It is not appropriate for the presider to be reading along in a missalette or to be gazing out into the assembly during the proclamation of the Word.

Responsorial Psalm

- After a period of silent reflection on the Word, the presider joins the assembly in singing the responsorial psalm.

Gospel Acclamation

- The Gospel acclamation is sung before the proclamation of the Gospel. During the Gospel acclamation, the presider moves to the ambo.

Gospel

- A deacon proclaims the Gospel in the usual manner. A layperson omits the greeting, "The Lord be with you," before reading the Gospel.

- While announcing the Gospel passage, the Gospel reader makes the sign of the cross on the book, then on the forehead, lips, and breast.

- At the end, the Gospel reader adds, "The Gospel of the Lord," to which the people make their response. After saying, "The Gospel of the Lord," the Gospel reader should wait until the people make their response, "Praise to you, Lord Jesus Christ," before kissing the book.

- Then the Gospel reader kisses the Gospel book and says inaudibly, "May the words of the Gospel wipe away our sins."

Homily

- A presider who is a deacon gives a homily. When the presider is a layperson who has not been delegated to preach, the pastor may prepare a homily to be read during the celebration. In other cases, when a layperson has been delegated to preach by the bishop, he or she may give those present a brief explanation of the biblical text, so that they may understand through faith the meaning of the celebration. After the homily, there may be a period of silence for reflection on the Word of God.

- After the homily, the deacon returns to the presidential chair, the layperson to his or her chair.

Dismissal of the Catechumens

- If holy communion is to be distributed and there are catechumens present, the SCAP provides several options for their dismissal.

Profession of Faith

- The creed is recited as at Mass.

General Intercessions

- The presider introduces the prayers of the faithful by inviting the community to intercede for all God's people.

- The presider gives a brief introduction that is addressed to the people, not to God.

- The intercessions are announced by someone other than the presider: cantor, reader, or one of the faithful. The intercessions should include prayers: 1) for the church, 2) for public authorities, 3) for those oppressed by any need, and 4) for the local community.

- The presider then concludes the prayers of the faithful with one of the prayers found in SCAP.

Act of Thanksgiving

- The presider then invites all to an act of thanksgiving, in which the people praise the glory and mercy of God. This may take the form of a psalm, canticle, hymn, litany of praise, or a prayer.

- In order to avoid all confusion between the eucharistic prayer of the Mass and the prayer of thanksgiving used in these Sunday celebrations, these prayers of thanksgiving are not to take the form of a eucharistic prayer or preface.

- If communion is to be shared, the communion rite follows.

- If communion is not to be shared, the concluding rite is preceded by the Lord's Prayer.

Communion Rite

- The presider then goes to the tabernacle, takes the vessel containing the consecrated bread, places it on the altar, and genuflects.

Lord's Prayer/Sign of Peace

- A presider who is a layperson returns to his or her chair and introduces the Lord's Prayer and the sign of peace. After the sign of peace the layperson returns to the altar for the invitation to communion. A presider who is a deacon remains at the altar for the Lord's Prayer and the Sign of Peace.

Invitation to Communion

- The presider genuflects, takes the consecrated bread, shows it to the people, and recites the invitation to communion.

Communion

- The presider then receives communion and is assisted by others, if necessary, in sharing communion with members of the assembly. After communion, if any consecrated bread remains, it is placed in the tabernacle. A period of silence may be observed or a song of praise may be sung.

Prayer after Communion

- The presider then returns to the chair and says the prayer after communion.

Concluding Rite

- The concluding rite includes the announcements, the collection of the monetary offerings of the assembly, the blessing, and dismissal.

- Announcements concerning parish life and activities may be made, but they should be kept brief.

- A presider who is a deacon says, "The Lord be with you," and then blesses the people.

- A presider who is not a deacon makes the sign of the cross on himself or herself while saying, "May the Lord bless us, protect us from evil, and bring us to everlasting life."

- The presider then dismisses the people.

- If there was an entrance procession of the ministers, it would be appropriate for the ministers to leave in procession.

7. Liturgy of the Word with Children

The *Directory for Masses with Children* (DMC) highlights the importance of the proclamation of God's Word in liturgical celebrations with children. Since Christ is present in the proclamation of the Word, it is important that God's Word be proclaimed in such a way that all who hear might take the message to heart. For this reason, the *Lectionary for Masses with Children* (LMC) was approved by the National Conference of Catholic Bishops for use at liturgical celebrations with children in the United States. LMC adapts the selection and arrangement of the readings of the lectionary so that children of catechetical age might be properly formed by the Word of God.

Both DMC and LMC indicate the appropriateness of a separate Liturgy of the Word for children at Masses with adults in which children also participate. After gathering with the main assembly for the introductory rites, the presider[1] formally sends the children and their ministers to a separate place where they will celebrate the Liturgy of the Word. At the conclusion of the Liturgy of the Word, the children then return to their families for the celebration of the Eucharist. The goal of a separate Liturgy of the Word with children is not to provide catechetical instruction for the children or to separate noisy children from the adult assembly but to provide an opportunity for the children to hear and reflect on the Word of God as it is addressed to them.

---

1 To distinguish between the one who presides at Mass and the one who presides at a separate Liturgy of the Word with children, this chapter will use the term "presider" for the priest at Mass and "leader" for the person who presides at Liturgy of the Word with children.

The Structure of Liturgy of the Word with Children

- **Introductory Rites:** The introductory rites include the procession from the main assembly, the entrance into the sacred space, and a focusing moment to help the children prepare to listen to the Word of God.

- **Liturgy of the Word**: The Liturgy of the Word includes one or two readings, the psalm response, the Gospel, a homily or a reflection on the Word of God, the profession of faith, and the prayers of the faithful.

- **Return to the Main Assembly**

The Leader's Role at Liturgy of the Word with Children

The leader's role is to facilitate the proclamation of God's Word to the children and to help the children respond to the Word of God in their lives. It is important for the leader to keep in mind that Liturgy of the Word is first and foremost a liturgical celebration. The space should be arranged so that the Word of God can be enthroned in a prominent place. If at all possible, a classroom should be avoided so as not to confuse the celebration of the liturgy with religious formation. The leader's chair should be placed in a prominent place so that it can be seen as a symbol of the role of leading the children in prayer. A candle may be prepared as a symbol of honor to the Word of God that enlightens us. If a classroom must be used, every effort should be made to transform the space from an educational environment into a sacred space, a place for prayer. Rather than having children seated at desks, chairs might be rearranged in a circle around the ambo or table where the Word is enthroned.

Since the leader's role is to facilitate the prayer of the children, it would be helpful to have another adult or some older children present to help move the children and to help maintain a sense of order. It is not appropriate for the leader to act as a disciplinarian. Within the liturgy, the leader should be assisted by other ministers to proclaim the readings and lead the singing. While there may be circumstances when there are no other ministers and the leader has to function alone, this should not be the norm.

Planning and Preparing for Liturgy of the Word with Children

Prior to the celebration of the liturgy, there are a number of responsibilities that the leader should assume. This includes both long-term planning and immediate preparation for the liturgy. While there may be a liturgy coordinator in the parish who is responsible for some of these details, it is the leader's ultimate responsibility to be certain that all is in order for the celebration of the liturgy.

Long-term planning of Liturgy of the Word with children includes:

- meeting with the liturgy team to contextualize the celebration within the Sunday Mass and within the overall liturgical plan for the seasons of the church year;

- meeting with the musicians to select music for the liturgy;

- coordinating the roles of other liturgical ministers.

Immediate preparation for the liturgy includes:

- preparing the liturgical space;

- coordinating the other liturgical ministers;

- selecting the liturgical texts;

- preparing a leader's book if needed. This book might be used for the focusing moment, the profession of faith, and the prayers of the faithful. A sample page for the presider's book is provided in Appendix B. Missalettes and loose leaf sheets are not appropriate;

- placing the children's lectionary at the ambo before Mass.

Introductory Rites

Sending forth from the main assembly

- The role of the presider at Mass is to send the children forth. LMC provides two examples of words that may be spoken by the presider in sending forth the children. If the presider chooses to use words "similar" to those found in the lectionary, they should be brief and to the point. This is not the time for a mini-homily. The presider then hands the children's lectionary to the person who will lead the Liturgy of the Word with children. Taking the children's lectionary the leader holds the book high and leads the children to the space for the children's celebration. The main assembly may sing an acclamation as the children leave; for example, "Send forth the children of God, let them hear the Good News."

Coming into the sacred space

- As the leader comes into the place for the proclamation of the Liturgy of the Word with children, the leader may continue to hold the book as the children enter, or the leader may immediately enthrone the lectionary on the ambo or table set up to hold the book.

- If the candle has not been lighted beforehand, the leader might light the candle at this point.

- Once all have reached their places, the leader then takes a chair that has been set up for the leader. It is not appropriate for the leader to sit on the floor.

Focusing

- It may be appropriate for the leader to speak a brief word to the children to help them focus on what they are about to do.

- This is not to be a second opening prayer.

- The leader's words should be very brief. For example, "Dear children, let us ask the Lord to open our hearts to hear God's Word." Since the leader is addressing the children, it is important for the leader to look at the children while talking to them.

Liturgy of the Word

- While the first (and second) reading is proclaimed by a reader, the leader's role is to focus attention on the proclamation of the Word.

- The leader needs to remember to set a good example for the children in listening to God's Word.

- After the readings there should be a period of silence for all to reflect on the words of Scripture.

Response/Gospel Acclamation

- As at Mass, a sung responsory should follow the first reading, and a Gospel acclamation should precede the Gospel. The leader should join the assembly in following the lead of the cantor.

- The music chosen should be simple, so that there is no need to rehearse beforehand. While the responsorial psalm may be recited, the Gospel acclamation is always to be sung (or else it is omitted).

- During the Gospel acclamation, the Gospel reader moves into place for the proclamation of the Gospel.

Gospel

- If a deacon is leading Liturgy of the Word with children, the deacon reads the Gospel. If a layperson is leading Liturgy of the Word with children, the leader or another reader may proclaim the Gospel.

- All stand for the Gospel reading.

- A deacon proclaims the Gospel in the usual manner. A layperson omits the greeting, "The Lord be with you," before reading the Gospel.

- While announcing the Gospel passage, the Gospel reader makes the sign of the cross on the book, then on the forehead, lips, and breast.

- At the end, the Gospel reader adds, "The Gospel of the Lord," to which the people make their response. After saying, "The Gospel of the Lord," the Gospel reader should wait until the people make their response, "Praise to you, Lord Jesus Christ," before kissing the book. Then the Gospel reader kisses the Gospel book and says inaudibly, "May the words of the Gospel wipe away our sins."

Homily

- A priest or deacon may preach a homily to the children, or one of the adults participating in the celebration may speak to the children after the Gospel.

- After the homily, there may be a period of silence for reflection on the Word of God.

Profession of Faith

- The leader then invites the children to stand and profess their faith.

- Either the Apostles' Creed or the Nicene Creed may be used. All may recite the creed together, or the leader may question the children, to which they respond "I do."[2]

General Intercessions

- The leader introduces the prayers of the faithful by inviting the children to intercede for all God's people.

- The leader gives a brief introduction that is addressed to the children, not to God. The intercessions are announced by someone other than the leader (cantor, reader, or one of the faithful), or the leader may invite the children to mention their intentions. The intercessions should include prayers: 1) for the church, 2) for public authorities, 3) for those oppressed by any need, and 4) for the local community.

- The leader then concludes the prayers of the faithful. The following structure and example is given as a model for this prayer:

STRUCTURE	EXAMPLE
You	God our creator,
who	you always hear the prayer of your people.
do	Open our hearts to receive the answer you give us
through	through Christ our Lord.
	Amen.

---

2 See the Creed in Appendix B.

Return to the Main Assembly

- After the prayers of the faithful, the children return to the main assembly for the Liturgy of the Eucharist.

- The leader should process in front of the children back to the main assembly. The leader should not return carrying the lectionary. It is best left where it was enthroned for the Liturgy of the Word with children.

- As the children return, they may accompany the procession of gifts, or they may simply return to their places as they arrive back in the main assembly.

- An adult should be the last one to leave after extinguishing the candle.

8. Order of Christian Funerals

Through the celebration of the church's funeral rites, Christians commend the faithful departed to God's tender and merciful love. The liturgies provide the opportunity to praise God and to offer thanksgiving for the gift of a life that has now returned to God. The funeral rites also seek to bring hope and consolation to the living, as the church proclaims the Lord's triumph over sin and death. There are three primary liturgical rites within *Order of Christian Funerals* (OCF): the vigil for the deceased, the funeral liturgy, and the rite of committal. Three other rites are also provided and may be used on occasions of prayer with the family: prayers after death, gathering in the presence of the body, and transfer of the body to the church or the place of committal.

The Vigil for the Deceased

The vigil for the deceased is the principal rite celebrated in the time following death before the funeral liturgy (or if there is no liturgy, before the Rite of Committal). At the vigil, the Christian community keeps watch with the family. It is the first occasion among the funeral rites for the solemn reading of God's Word. Consoled by the Word of God, the assembly calls on the Father of all mercy to receive the deceased into the kingdom of light and peace.

The vigil may take the form either of a Liturgy of the Word or of some part of the Liturgy of the Hours for the dead. Two services are provided in the rite: vigil for the deceased, and vigil for the deceased with reception in the church. The second service is used when the vigil is celebrated in the church.

The vigil may be celebrated in the home of the deceased, in the funeral home, in the church, or in some other suitable place. Adaptations of the vigil may be made depending on where the celebration occurs.

The vigil in the form of the Liturgy of the Word consists of the introductory rites, the Liturgy of the Word, the prayers of intercession, and a concluding rite.

As a liturgical rite, special emphasis should be given to the participation of the faithful. Besides the presiding minister, other ministers should exercise their liturgical roles. A reader should proclaim the Word of God. A cantor should lead the singing, since music is integral to all liturgical celebrations. In the choice of music, preference should be given to singing the opening song and the responsorial psalm. The litany, the Lord's Prayer, and a closing song may also be sung.

Preparing for the Celebration

- Priests, as teachers of faith and ministers of comfort, preside at the funeral rites. When no priest is available, deacons, as ministers of the Word, preside at funeral rites. When no priest or deacon is available, a layperson presides.

- The presiding minister should vest according to local custom. If the vigil is celebrated in the church, a priest or deacon who presides wears an alb and stole.

- The presider needs to prepare for the vigil by choosing the readings and the prayers that fit the deceased and the occasion of death. Part V of the ritual contains additional texts that may be used in the rite.

- Appropriate music should be chosen by the musician and the presider to support the family and to affirm hope in the resurrection.

Introductory Rites

Greeting

- The presiding minister greets those present with one of the formularies found in the ritual text.

- The rite does not indicate beginning with the sign of the cross.

- The greeting is meant to be a formal exchange between the presider and the assembly, who mutually acknowledge Christ's presence in their midst (for example, "May the Father of mercies, the God of all consolation, be with you"). For this reason, it is not appropriate to greet the assembly with a merely human exchange (for example, "Good evening").

- As the presider voices the greeting, the presider should make eye contact with the members of the assembly. The presider should sustain eye contact while the assembly makes its response.

Opening Song

- The celebration continues with a song.

- A worship aid or hymnal should be provided to facilitate singing and participation by the assembly.

Invitation to Prayer/Opening Prayer

- After the presider invites all to prayer, all pray silently for a while. Then the presider says the opening prayer.

- The presider should choose a prayer from the ritual that best fits the deceased and the occasion of death.

Liturgy of the Word

Biblical Readings

- During the readings, the presider attends to the proclamation of the Word.

- The presider sets the example for the assembly by focusing attention on the proclamation of the Word.

- It is never appropriate for the presider to be reading along in a missalette or to be gazing out into the assembly during the proclamation of the Word.

- If there is no reader, the presider may proclaim the first reading.

Responsorial Psalm

- After a period of silent reflection on the Word, the presider joins the assembly in singing the responsorial psalm.

Gospel

- The Gospel reading is then proclaimed.

- A priest or deacon proclaims the Gospel in the usual manner. A layperson omits the greeting, "The Lord be with you," before reading the Gospel.

- While announcing the Gospel passage, the Gospel reader makes the sign of the cross on the book, then on the forehead, lips, and breast.

- At the end, the Gospel reader adds, "The Gospel of the Lord," to which the people make their response. After saying, "The Gospel of the Lord," the Gospel reader should wait until the people make their response, "Praise to you, Lord Jesus Christ," before kissing the book.

Homily

- A priest or deacon gives a homily. When a layperson has been delegated to preach by the bishop, he or she may give those present a brief explanation of the biblical text, so that they may understand through faith the meaning of the celebration.

Prayers of Intercession

- The presider leads one of the litanies, invites the faithful to pray the Lord's Prayer, and prays the concluding prayer.

- After the concluding prayer, the presider may invite a member or a friend of the family to speak in remembrance of the deceased. This addition to the rite can be a very appropriate moment of comfort and healing for the family and friends of the deceased. The presider might invite the assembly to see the connection between the story of God's love as proclaimed in the Scriptures and the story of the deceased as told in the words of remembrance.

Concluding Rite

Blessing

- Before the blessing, the presider may trace the sign of the cross on the forehead of the deceased while saying the words, "Eternal rest...."

- The presider blesses those present with the appropriate formulary.

- A priest or deacon blesses the people, making the sign of the cross over them.

- A layperson invokes God's blessing and signs himself or herself with the sign of the cross.

- The ritual does not include a formal dismissal, since members of the family and friends often stay and continue visitation.

- If all will depart, it might be appropriate for the presider to add, "Let us go in peace," to which all respond, "Thanks be to God."

Gestures

- The OCF makes no reference to the leader extending hands during the prayers. Perhaps this is because it is assumed that the presider would have the ritual book in hand and would not be able to extend hands in prayer.

- If there is a server or an assistant present to assist the leader by holding the book, it might be appropriate for the leader to extend hands when praying the opening prayer, the Lord's Prayer, and the concluding prayer.

- When the presider is a priest or deacon, it might be appropriate to extend hands when greeting the people in the introductory rites and before the Gospel.

Funeral Liturgy

The funeral liturgy is the central liturgical celebration of the Christian community for the deceased. Here the community gathers with the family and friends of the deceased to give praise and thanks to God for Christ's victory over sin and death, and to commend the deceased to God's mercy. There are two forms of the funeral liturgy: the funeral Mass, and the funeral liturgy outside Mass. The funeral Mass includes the reception of the body (if this has not already occurred), the celebration of the Liturgy of the Word, the Liturgy of the Eucharist, and the final commendation and farewell. The funeral liturgy outside Mass includes all these elements except the Liturgy of the Eucharist.

The priest is the ordinary minister who presides at the funeral liturgy. When a priest is not available, the deacon may preside at the funeral liturgy outside Mass. Whenever possible, ministers should include the family in planning the funeral liturgy: in the choice of readings, prayers and music for the liturgy, and in the designation of ministers. The family should be encouraged to assist in placing the pall or other Christian symbols on the coffin during the rite of reception.

Introductory Rites

- Unless the rite of reception already took place, the introductory rites include the reception of the body of the deceased.

Greeting

- The presider and other ministers go to the door of the church and greet those present using one of the formularies of the rite.

- The rite does not indicate beginning with the sign of the cross.

- The greeting of the Mass is meant to be a formal exchange between the presider and the assembly, who mutually acknowledge Christ's presence in their midst (for example, "May the Father of mercies, the God of all consolation, be with you"). For this reason, it is not appropriate to greet the assembly with a merely human exchange (for example, "Good morning").

- As the presider voices the greeting, the presider should make eye contact with members of the assembly. The presider should sustain eye contact while the assembly makes its response.

Sprinkling with Holy Water

- The presider then sprinkles the coffin with holy water, reciting the formula found in the ritual text.

Placing of the Pall

- If it is the custom of the local community, the pall is then placed on the coffin by family members.

- The pall is a reminder of the deceased's baptism into Christ Jesus. As an important Christian symbol, it should never be replaced by a flag or other covering. If the coffin is covered with a flag when the coffin is brought to the church, it should be removed and replaced with the pall.

Entrance Procession

- The presider and other ministers precede the coffin and the mourners into church. During the procession, a psalm, hymn, or responsory is sung.

- A symbol of the Christian life, such as the Book of Gospels, a Bible, or a cross may be carried in procession, then placed on the coffin, either in silence or with a text from the funeral ritual.

- On reaching the altar, the presider makes a deep bow to the altar (in the presence of the tabernacle, the ministers genuflect), kisses the altar, and goes to the presidential chair.

Opening Prayer

- When all have reached their places, the presider invites all to pray. After a brief period of silent prayer, the presider says the opening prayer.

- Since the funeral rite has its own introductory rites, the penitential rite is omitted.

Liturgy of the Word

- At the funeral Mass, the Liturgy of the Word is celebrated in the usual manner with the biblical readings, responsorial psalm, Gospel acclamation, and general intercessions.

- At the funeral liturgy outside Mass, the Liturgy of the Word is celebrated as above. Following the concluding prayer to the general intercessions, the presider invites all to pray the Lord's Prayer.

Liturgy of the Eucharist

- At the funeral Mass, the Liturgy of the Eucharist is celebrated in the usual manner.

- If incense is used at the preparation of the altar and gifts, the body is not incensed at this time.

- At the funeral liturgy outside Mass, the Liturgy of the Eucharist is omitted; however, the celebration may include holy communion.

Final Commendation

- The presider and other ministers go to a place near the body. Assisting ministers carry the censer and holy water, if these are to be used.

Invitation to prayer

- After the presider invites the assembly to prayer, all pray silently for a while.

Signs of Farewell

- The presider may now use holy water and/or incense. If the body has been sprinkled with holy water during the rite of reception at the beginning of the funeral liturgy, the sprinkling is ordinarily omitted.

Song of Farewell

- The song of farewell is then sung. It may be sung before, during, or after the sprinkling and incensing of the body.

- It seems most appropriate to have the song of farewell accompany the sign of farewell.

Prayer of Commendation

- The presider then says one of the prayers of commendation.

Procession to the place of committal

- An assisting minister, or, in the absence of an assisting minister, the presider says, "In peace let us take our brother/sister to his/her place of rest."

- If a symbol of the Christian life has been placed on the coffin, it is removed at this time. If it belongs to the family, it is returned with reverence at this time.

- The procession then begins with the ministers preceding the coffin. The family and mourners follow. A song may be sung during the procession.

Rite of Committal

The rite of committal, the conclusion of the funeral rites, is the final act of the community of faith in caring for the body of its deceased member. Whenever possible, the rite should be celebrated at the site of committal, that is, beside the open grave or place of interment, rather than at a cemetery chapel. Two forms of the rite are provided: the rite of committal and the rite of committal with final commendation. The first form is used when the final commendation is celebrated as part of the conclusion of the funeral liturgy. The second form is used when the final commendation does not take place during the funeral liturgy or when no funeral liturgy precedes the committal rite.

Both forms of the committal rite begin with an invitation, Scripture verse, and prayer over the place of committal. The rite of committal continues with the words of committal, the intercessions, and the Lord's Prayer. The rite of committal with final commendation continues with an invitation to prayer, a pause for silent prayer, the sprinkling and incensing of the body, the song of farewell, and the prayer of commendation. Both forms conclude with a prayer over the people, which includes the verse, "Eternal Rest...," and a blessing. A song may be sung, and a final gesture of leave-taking may be made.

Invitation

- When the funeral procession arrives at the place of committal, the minister invites all to prayer.

Scripture Verse

- The presider reads a brief Scripture verse, introducing the text with the words, "We read in sacred Scripture...."

Prayer over the Place of Committal

- The several alternatives of the prayer take into account whether the grave or resting place has already been blessed and situations in which the final disposition of the body will actually take place at a later time.

Committal

- The minister then says the words of committal.

Final Commendation

- See description of final commendation, pages 137-38, if the final commendation is to be performed at the site of committal.

Intercessions

- The presider introduces the intercessions. An assisting minister may read the petitions.

The Lord's Prayer/Concluding Prayer

- The presider invites all to pray the Lord's Prayer, and then prays the concluding prayer.

Prayer over the People

- The presider, with hands outstretched, says the prayer over the people.

- With hands closed, the presider says the "Eternal rest…."

- The presider gives the blessing according to the rite.

- The presider then concludes by dismissing the people.

- A final song may be sung.

When possible, families might be invited to remain at the grave site until the body is lowered into the ground. Where it is the custom, some sign or gesture of leave taking may be made (for example, placing flowers or soil on the grave).

A Formation Process for Presiders

Based on the insights of this book that identify a number of attitudes and skills needed by those who lead liturgical prayer, this appendix describes a process that can be used by those who are responsible for the formation of presiders. The methodology of this process is based on the insights of Thomas Groome, who proposes a model for adult learning that he describes as shared Christian praxis.[1]

Groome's model suggests that learners need to be personally involved as participants in the educational process. After reflecting on their own experience, entering into conversation with others, and acknowledging the wisdom of the Christian tradition, learners are invited to personally and critically appropriate the faith.[2] Throughout his model, Groome emphasizes the importance of educating for wisdom, rather than simply for cognition. He underscores the belief that education involves the whole person and not only the mind. This holistic understanding of Christian formation suggests a way of "being" in the world, a way of living Christian faith, rather than simply a way to acquire knowledge. As such, Groome's approach of shared

---

1 Groome defines shared Christian praxis as "a participative pedagogy in which people reflect critically on their own historical agency in time and place and on their own sociocultural reality, have access together to Christian Story/Vision, and personally appropriate it in community with the creative intent of renewed praxis in Christian faith toward God's reign for all creation" (133).

2 As used here, the term "Christian tradition" includes the teachings of Scripture and the Magisterium of the Church as well as the established local traditions that have developed through the interpretation of church teaching.

praxis is much more a continual process than a step-by-step approach for acquiring knowledge.

Because effective presiding involves much more than simply acquiring knowledge about presiding, Groome's model can be applied appropriately to the formation process for presiders described below. In addition, this formation process will employ the use of mystagogical reflection, modeling and mentoring as part of the learning experience. An outline and a detailed description of the process follow.

Step I: Identifying the Assembly As the Context for the Ministry of Presiding

- focusing on the liturgical assembly through a common experience

- reflecting on the experience of being a member of the assembly

- studying the Christian tradition with regard to the assembly

- correlating the praxis experience to the Christian tradition

Step II: Examining the Presider's Role within the Assembly

- focusing on the presider's role through a common experience

- reflecting on the role of the presider from the assembly's perspective

- studying the Christian tradition with regard to the role of the presider

- correlating the praxis experience to the Christian tradition

Step III: Identifying the Attitudes and Skills Needed by the Presider

- focusing on the attitudes and skills of the presider as experienced through several liturgical celebrations

- reflecting on these attitudes and skills in light of the worship experience

- studying the Christian tradition with regard to the presider's attitudes and skills

- correlating the experience to the Christian tradition

Step IV: Developing a Presidential Style

- developing a style of presiding in light of reflection/ study/correlation in Steps I-III

- presiding in small groups followed by reflection on the experience of presiding

Step V: Presiding within the Liturgical Assembly

- presiding within the liturgical assembly

- mystagogical reflection on the experience of presiding

Setting

The setting for the use of this process is a group of learners who are in the process of preparing to preside at liturgical celebrations. In addition to the group of learners, there is a leader who is experienced in presiding who will serve as both facilitator and resource person for the group.[3]

As facilitator, you will guide the reflection process throughout the learning experience and will assist the learners in making the correla-

---

3 In the remainder of this appendix, the formation process will be presented by direct instructions for the leader, who will be addressed as "you."

tions between their personal reflections and the Christian tradition. As a resource person, you will offer input with regard to the Christian tradition and the liturgical traditions of the church.[4] Your role also includes creating a setting and an atmosphere conducive to adult learning.[5]

Step I: Identifying the Assembly As the Context for the Ministry of Presiding

The goal of the first step is to help the learners identify the assembly as a primary liturgical symbol and as the context for shaping the ministry of the presider. In this step, you will help the learners to focus attention on their experience of the liturgy as members of the assembly. In order to facilitate this process, you might provide a model of effective presiding so that the learners would have a common experience of the liturgy on which to base their reflections. Following the liturgical experience, invite the learners to describe their role as members of the assembly within the liturgy:

- As members of the assembly, what was their role?

- What did they do within the liturgy?

- Were they actively engaged in the liturgy?

- Were they participants or spectators?

- What were the most important parts of the liturgy?

---

4   Part One of this book is intended to be a model and resource for the first three steps of this methodology.

5   Groome suggests that an appropriate environment for adult learning is one that is conducive to participation, partnership, and dialogue. These three elements help to create a hospitable learning environment that reflects and nurtures a growing level of trust where learning can take place. Groome also suggests that the physical environment needs to be prepared to enhance participation, partnership, and dialogue. For example, seating should be arranged so that participants can see one another and enter into dialogue with each other. See Groome 168-170.

- Who did them?

- What did the assembly do while the other ministers functioned?

After the learners describe their role as members of the assembly, invite them to reflect critically on the meaning of their named experience:

- What was the meaning of the assembly's role in the liturgy? How was this shown?

- Were the members of the assembly drawn into the celebration as active participants? How was this shown?

- What was the relation between the assembly and the other ministers? How was this shown?

- How significant was the role of the assembly within the liturgy?

Following the process of reflection, challenge the learners to study the Christian tradition to see what insights can be learned about the liturgical assembly. Invite them to examine the official liturgical texts to see what is said about the role of the assembly within the liturgy.[6] In addition, help to make accessible the history and various liturgical traditions of the church with regard to the role of the assembly within the liturgy.

After their study of the role of the assembly in the liturgy, encourage the learners to make a correlation between their reflections and their study of the role of the assembly within the liturgy. Here, you should help the learners draw from their own experience and from the traditions of the church to see the assembly as a primary liturgical symbol, and as the context for shaping all other liturgical ministries, including their own ministry as presiders.

---

6 Chapter 1 provides an example of how a study of select liturgical documents reveals the assembly as a primary liturgical symbol and the context for shaping all other liturgical ministries.

Step II: Examining the Presider's Role within the Assembly

Step II begins by drawing on the insights that the learners have gained from Step I. After they successfully recognize the assembly as the context for shaping the presider's ministry, invite them to focus on the presider's role within the assembly. Encourage them to draw on their common experience of the liturgy to name and describe the role of the presider in relation to the assembly:

- What did the presider do?

- How did the presider relate to the assembly?

- How did the presider relate to the other liturgical ministers?

- What did the presider do when other ministers were functioning?

After describing the role of the presider from their perspective as members of the assembly, challenge the learners to reflect critically on their description:

- What impact did the presider have on the worshiping community? How was this shown?

- Did the presider respect the primacy of the assembly? How was this shown?

- Did the presider invite the assembly to full, conscious, and active participation? How was this shown?

- Did the presider respect the ministry of others? How was this shown?

In this step, it might be helpful for you to provide a model of ineffective presiding to contrast with the learners' experience of effective presiding. This could help the learners in the reflection process to see the impact of the presider on the worshiping community (see MCW 6).

Following the process of reflection, invite the learners to study the Christian tradition to see what insights they can learn about the role of the presider in relation to the assembly. Have the learners examine the liturgical texts themselves to see what is said about the presider's role.[7] In addition, help to make accessible the history and traditions of the presider's role in relation to the assembly.

After a study of the presider's role and its relation to the assembly, encourage the learners to make a correlation between their personal reflections and their study of the presider's ministry within the liturgy. Here, you can help them draw from their own experience and from the traditions of the church to see the presider's role in relation to the assembly.[8] Specifically, you must help the learners come to understand that the ministry of the presider is one of service within the liturgical assembly; that the presider is called to animate the prayer of the community and to coordinate the various other liturgical ministries; that the presider must learn to work with others in creating an environment for worship.

Step III: Identifying the Attitudes and Skills Needed by the Presider

The third step builds on the insights that the learners have gained from the previous two steps concerning the primacy of the assembly and the presider's role in relation to the assembly. Here, invite the learners to draw on their common experiences of the liturgy (effective and ineffective modeling) to name and describe the attitudes and skills that they see operative within an effective presider:

- What attitudes in the presider reflect the presider's attention to the assembly as a primary symbol within the liturgy?

---

7 Chapter 2 provides an example of how a study of select liturgical documents describes the role of the presider in relation to the assembly.

8 See the summary at the conclusion of Chapter 2.

- What attitudes reflect and foster a sense of care for the assembly and its members?

- What attitudes reflect the presider's ability to work with the other liturgical ministers?

- What attitudes reflect the presider's understanding of this role within the liturgy?

- What skills does the presider manifest in the celebration of the liturgy?

- What skills are operative as the presider leads the assembly in prayer?

- What skills does the presider manifest in relating to the assembly and to the other liturgical ministers?

- What skills does the presider need to develop further?

After the learners describe the attitudes and skills they see operative, invite them to reflect critically on the attitudes and skills they see as important in an effective presider:

- How does a presider manifest these attitudes and skills?

- What happens when these attitudes and skills are not present?

- How does one develop these attitudes and skills?

Following their critical reflection, present the Christian tradition to see what further insights can be learned concerning the attitudes and skills needed by the presider.[9] Specifically, you would address the need for the presider to manifest attitudes of hospitality, reverence, and authenticity in the exercise of the presider's ministry. You might also emphasize the importance of the presider acquiring the skills of leading public prayer and the skills of working with others in the

---

9 Chapters 3 and 4 provide a description of a number of skills and attitudes needed by an effective presider.

planning and celebration of the liturgy. You could also suggest the importance of ongoing theological reflection as one of the ways a presider can continue developing in this ministry.[10]

After a study of the Christian tradition with regard to the attitudes and skills needed by the presider, invite the learners to make a correlation between the reflection on their experience and the Christian tradition. This correlation prepares the learners to move on to the next step, where they will have the opportunity to cultivate the attitudes and to practice the skills needed for presiding.

Step IV: Developing a Presidential Style

Here, you will actively engage the learners in the process of developing their own style of presiding. Having identified a number of key attitudes needed by the presider, the learners now need to make a conscious effort to develop these attitudes as they practice the skills of leading public prayer and working collaboratively with others.[11]

In this step, each learner practices both the techniques of prayer, as well as the actual prayers and actions of the liturgy. The learners work in small groups as they seek to develop the attitudes and skills needed for leading public prayer.[12] Provide each learner with several oppor-

---

10 Throughout the five steps of the methodology, the learners have the opportunity to develop the skill of theological reflection. Part of your responsibility is to help them sharpen their skill of theological reflection from the beginning of the process, to challenge them to reflect critically on their experience, and to evaluate the correlation of the reflection on their experience with their study of the Christian tradition.

11 While it is possible to practice the skills of leading public prayer and working with others, it is much more difficult to practice attitudes like hospitality, reverence, and authenticity. These attitudes are cultivated by a conscious reflection on the demands of the attitudes, followed by a conscious decision to incorporate these attitudes while practicing the skills of leading prayer and working with others.

12 Given the significant differences in ritual dynamics and styles between small and large groups, alert the learners to changes that will be required when they move into larger assemblies, especially in the next step. For example, the learners will need to be attentive to the size of the worship space and the location of the assembly within the worship space as they learn to adapt their gestures and voice to fit the space.

tunities to lead the group in prayer, first in practicing prayer techniques and later in practicing the liturgical texts of the liturgy. After each session of leading the group, encourage the learner who presided to reflect on the experience of leading prayer:

- What did the presider do?
- How effectively did the presider lead the community in prayer?
- How did the presider exemplify the attitudes of hospitality, reverence, and authenticity?

Then invite the learner's peers to offer commendations and recommendations with regard to the presider's ministry:

- What attitudes did the presider exemplify?
- What skills has the presider already developed?
- What attitudes and skills need further development?

In addition, provide the opportunity for the learners to work with mentors who will guide them in developing their presidential style. From their own experience as presiders, the mentors can both offer encouragement and challenge the learners as they work to cultivate the attitudes and skills needed for presiding.

This step of developing a presidential style could also include each learner making one or two videotapes. Each learner would then review the videotape with you, the mentor, or both. This experience would provide the learner an opportunity to see the presidential style that is taking shape, and to evaluate how well the learner is developing the skills of prayer leadership and incorporating the attitudes of hospitality, reverence, and authenticity as the learner moves through the experience.

It is also important to provide the learners with the opportunity to work with others in the actual planning and celebration of a liturgy for the entire group. This activity will challenge the learners to work collaboratively in the learning process. The mentor might also be able to provide additional opportunities for the learner to work with others in preparing different kinds of liturgical services.

By presiding, by participating as members of the assembly when others preside, and by reflection on their own practice and the practice of their peers, the learners are encouraged to continue to cultivate the attitudes and develop the skills that are needed as the learner prepares to preside within the liturgical assembly in Step V.

Because presiding is an art that involves the development of a number of attitudes and skills, it is important that the move from Step IV to Step V follow sufficient amount of time during which the learner works to develop the attitudes and skills that are necessary in this ministry. In addition, it seems that it is necessary to have some kind of evaluation process that would ensure that the learner is adequately prepared to move from practice to the actual experience of presiding.[13]

Step V: Presiding within the Liturgical Assembly

The final step of this pedagogical method moves the learner beyond the practice of presiding to the actual experience of presiding within the liturgical assembly followed by a process of mystagogical reflection.[14]

---

13 Your evaluation should include input from the learner, mentor, and peers on the basis of the videotape review and the varied experiences of presiding within the learning experience. This evaluation should include an assessment of the presider's ability to lead the community in prayer and to work with others in the planning and celebration of the liturgy. In addition to an evaluation of the technical skills required for effective presiding (e.g., knowledge and understanding of the rite, bodily ease, eye contact, facial expression, volume, pace, tone of voice, use of gesture, etc.), it is important to assess how well the learner has incorporated the attitudes of reverence, hospitality, and authenticity in manifesting an effective presidential style. You would seem to have the ultimate responsibility for commending the learner to the final step or recommending that the learner continue to work in this step to cultivate the attitudes and skills needed to be an effective presider.

14 A thorough discussion of the meaning of the term "mystagogy" can be found in Mazza. Mazza notes that "Nowadays, the term 'mystagogy' signifies catechetical instructions on the sacraments, with special reference to the sacraments of Christian

Quite often in moving to this step, the new presider moves beyond the formal learning environment. Once the learner begins to preside within the liturgical assembly, he or she needs to admit that presiding, like any art, requires ongoing practice, discipline, and the refinement of skills. For this reason, the final movement, presiding within the eucharistic assembly, must include a period of mystagogical reflection. Here, your role is to encourage the ongoing relationship between the new presider and the mentor. You might suggest that the mentor help the new presider reflect on the actual experience of presiding with all that this entails:

- How well did the presider work with others in the planning and celebration of the liturgy?

- How did the presider relate to the other liturgical ministers?

- What was the presider's relation to the assembly?

- How did the presider manifest the attitudes of hospitality, reverence, and authenticity throughout the liturgy?

In addition to the presider's own reflections and those of his or her mentor, encourage the new presider to elicit feedback from members of the assembly who are invited to offer commendations and recommendations on the presider's style:

- How did the presider relate to the assembly?

- How did the presider relate to the other liturgical ministers?

---

initiation and to the deeper spiritual meaning of the liturgical rites. The broader sense of mystagogy as meaning simply 'explanation of the rites' dates from the beginning of the Byzantine period. It is on the basis of this broader meaning that mystagogy is applied to every type of liturgical celebration, including priestly ordination and the anointing of the sick" (1). In this appendix, the term "mystagogy" is used to refer to the ongoing process of understanding the liturgy through a guided reflection on both the rites and the experience of presiding at the rites.

- How effective was the presider in leading the prayer of the community?

- What skills did the presider manifest?

- What skills does the presider need to improve?

- Was the presider hospitable, reverent, and authentic in his or her words and actions?

Mystagogical Reflection

By encouraging the use of mystagogical reflection, you will reinforce the understanding that presiding is an art that needs to be continually developed. One is not born a presider. Rather, one learns to be an effective presider through reflection on experience, study, cultivation of a number of attitudes and skills, and the actual experience of presiding. Inviting members of the assembly to assist in the process of ongoing reflection is one of the ways that the presider can continue to grow in developing the attitudes and skills needed to preside within the assembly.

Modeling

Modeling is a pedagogical technique that you can use throughout the learning process. By providing a number of models of effective and ineffective presiding, you will help the learners reflect on the impact of the presider on the assembly's experience of worship. Modeling also provides the opportunity for the learners to see in the models the attitudes and skills needed by an effective presider. In addition, the examples of effective presiding will provide the learners with models that the learners can imitate as they begin to develop their own style of presiding.[15]

---

15 Aidan Kavanagh notes that "mastery of liturgical service, like mastery of language, begins with imitation and continues to imitate long after one is on one's own, for it is nearly impossible to avoid imitating what is admirable" (95).

Mentoring

Mentoring is another tool that can be used throughout the learning experience.[16] Encourage each learner to choose a mentor who is experienced in presiding, and who is able to engage the learner in critical reflection on the experience of presiding. The role of the mentor is to assist the learner in the reflection process, especially in Step IV and Step V, when the learner begins to develop a presidential style. In addition, having the wisdom and support of an experienced presider can provide the learner with the encouragement needed to stretch beyond the learner's horizons in trying new styles and techniques in developing an effective presidential style.

Summary

Throughout the five steps of this method, your role is to invite the learners to name and reflect on their experiences, first as members of the assembly, and finally as presiders within the liturgical assembly. This process of naming and reflection, combined with study of the Christian tradition, will help to prepare the learners to make the necessary correlation between their experience and the traditions of the church as they begin to develop a style of presiding that reflects the attitudes and skills needed by one who presides in the midst of the assembly.

Paralleling the structure of the first part of this book, the first three steps of this methodology are designed to help beginning presiders:

1. to identify the assembly as the context for the ministry of presiding;

---

16 A detailed study of mentoring, including its theological foundations, pedagogical principles, and procedural guidelines, can be found in Jones. Jones notes that the mentor "is a teacher. He is a teacher whose task takes on the role of guide, which is much more than simply an instructor. While he may give instructions and relate information, his task goes beyond that. He must endeavor to help his trainees develop their own skills and proficiencies, gain insight and understanding, and become able to act upon that insight and understanding" (69-70).

2. to examine the presider's role within the liturgical
   assembly; and

3. to identify the attitudes and skills needed
   by the presider.

The final steps are designed to provide the opportunity for the beginning presider:

4. to develop a style of presiding that incorporates
   the attitudes and skills identified; and

5. to complete the experience of presiding within the
   liturgical assembly with a process of mystagogical
   reflection.

The basic structure of this model follows the approach from practical theology known as praxis-theory-praxis, which draws on the learner's experience as the starting point for the learning process. The process of reflection on experience is accompanied by a study of the Christian tradition as it relates to both the liturgical assembly and the ministry of the presider. The process is enhanced by the use of modeling and mentoring, which aid the learner in cultivating the attitudes and developing the skills necessary for presiding within the liturgical assembly. The actual experience of presiding within the liturgical assembly is completed by a period of mystagogical reflection, during which the presider continues to reflect on the experience of presiding.

Sample Page for Presider's Book

Focusing Moment

Brothers and Sisters,
Let us take a moment of silence to be aware of God's presence
    in our midst (pause).
Let us ask God to open our ears and our hearts to hear his
Word this day.

All are seated for the readings.

Creed

We stand to profess our faith in the God as we respond "I do."

Do you believe in God, our heavenly Father, who speaks to us
through his holy Word? (I do.)

Do you believe in Jesus, who came to show us how to follow
God's Word? (I do.)

Do you believe in the Holy Spirit, who helps us obey God's
Word in our lives? (I do.)

This is our faith, the faith of the Church. We are proud to
profess it through Christ, our Lord. (Amen.)

Prayers of the Faithful

God always hears our prayers, and so we pray:

1. For the church and for all members of God's family, we pray. (Hear us, O Lord.)

2. For the leaders of our country and for all world leaders, we pray. (Hear us, O Lord.)

3. For our families and neighbors, our friends and our enemies, we pray. (Hear us, O Lord.)

4. For those who are sick, and for those who have died, we pray. (Hear us, O Lord.)

God of Love, we ask you to hear our prayers.
Bless us and all people with the love of your Spirit.
Help us to live our lives in love for you and for each other.
We ask this through Christ, our Lord. (Amen.)

Works Cited

The Association of National Secretaries of Europe. *Leading the Prayer of God's People: Liturgical Presiding for Priests and Laity*. Dublin: The Columba Press, 1991.

Augustine. "Sermo CCLXXII." In *Patrologia Latina*. Patrologia Cursus Completus, Series Latina, vol. 38, ed. J. P. Migne. Paris: 1844.

Browning, Don S. *A Fundamental Practical Theology*. Minneapolis: Fortress Press, 1991.

Brueggemann, Walter. *The Prophetic Imagination*. Philadelphia: Fortress Press, 1978.

Casey, Thomas F. *Pastoral Manual for New Priests*. Milwaukee: The Bruce Publishing Co., 1962.

Ceremonial for the Use of the Catholic Churches in the United States of America, 8th revised ed. Philadelphia: H. L. Kilner & Co., 1894.

Chupungco, Ansgar. *Cultural Adaptation of the Liturgy*. New York: Paulist Press, 1982.

———. *Liturgies of the Future: The Process and Methods of Inculturation*. New York: Paulist Press, 1989.

Dallen, James. *The Dilemma of Priestless Sundays*. Chicago: Liturgy Training Publications, 1994.

Diekmann, Godfrey, OSB. Foreword to *Strong, Loving and Wise*, by Robert W. Hovda.

Empereur, James. "Presidential Style." In *The New Dictionary of Sacramental Worship*, edited by Peter E. Fink, 1006–1010. Collegeville, Minnesota: The Liturgical Press, 1990.

Fink, Peter E. "Reverence." In *The New Dictionary of Sacramental Worship*, edited by Peter E. Fink, 1098–1101. Collegeville, Minn.: The Liturgical Press, 1990.

Groome, Thomas. *Sharing Faith: A Comprehensive Approach to Religious Education and Pastoral Ministry*. San Francisco: Harper, 1991.

Works Cited

Harrington, Mary Therese. *A Place for All: Mental Retardation, Catechesis and Liturgy*. American Essays in Liturgy, ed. Edward Foley. Collegeville, Minnesota: The Liturgical Press, 1992.

Hiltner, Seward. *The Christian Shepherd: Some Aspects of Pastoral Care*. Nashville: Abingdon Press, 1959.

Hovda, Robert. "For Presiders/Preachers." In *Touchstones for Liturgical Ministers*, edited by Virginia Sloyan, 27–28. Washington, DC: The Liturgical Conference, 1978.

————. "The Primacy of the Ministry of the Assembly." In *The Assembly: A People Gathered in Your Name*. Milwaukee: Office of Worship, 1981.

————. *Strong, Loving and Wise*. Collegeville, Minnesota: The Liturgical Press, 1976.

Huck, Gabe. *Liturgy with Style and Grace*. 2nd ed. Chicago: Liturgy Training Publications, 1989.

Hughes, Kathleen. *Lay Presiding: The Art of Leading Prayer*. American Essays in Liturgy Series, ed. Edward Foley. Collegeville, Minnesota: The Liturgical Press, 1991.

————. "Sunday Worship in the Absence of a Priest: Some Disquieting Reflections." *New Theology Review* 8, no. 1 (1995): 45-57.

————. "Types of Prayer in the Liturgy." In *The New Dictionary of Sacramental Worship*, edited by Peter E. Fink, 959–67. Collegeville, Minnesota: The Liturgical Press, 1990.

International Commission on English in the Liturgy. *Documents on the Liturgy, 1963-1979: Conciliar, Papal, and Curial Texts*. Collegeville, Minn.: The Liturgical Press, 1982.

Jones, C. David. *The Pastoral Mentor*. Richmond, Virginia: Skipworth Press, Inc., 1980.

Kavanagh, Aidan. *Elements of Rite: A Handbook of Liturgical Style*. New York: Pueblo Publishing Co., 1982.

Keating, James. *The Priest: His Character and Work*. New York: Benziger Brothers, 1903.

Legrand, Hervé-Marie. "The Presidency of the Eucharist According to Ancient Tradition." *Worship* 53, no. 5 (1979): 413–438.

Maertens, Thierry. *Assembly for Christ*. English trans. London: Darton, Longman & Todd, 1970.

Malarcher, Willy. "Hospitality." In *The New Dictionary of Sacramental Worship*, edited by Peter E. Fink, 558–62. Collegeville, Minnesota: The Liturgical Press, 1990.

Martimort, Aimé-Georges. "The Assembly." In *Introduction to the Liturgy*. The Church at Prayer, vol. 1, edited by A. G. Martimort. New York: Desclee Company, 1968. Reprint edition edited by A. Flannery and V. Ryan, translated by Robert Fisher et al.

Martimort, Aimé-Georges. "The Assembly." In *Principles of the Liturgy*, rev. ed. The Church at Prayer, vol. 1, edited by A. G. Martimort, translated by Matthew O'Connell. Collegeville, Minnesota: The Liturgical Press, 1987).

Mazza, Enrico. *Mystagogy: A Theology of Liturgy in the Patristic Age*. New York: Pueblo Publishing Co., 1989.

NCCB Bishops' Committee on the Liturgy. "The Assembly in Christian Worship." *Newsletter* (Sept 1977).

Nouwen, Henri. "Hospitality." *Monastic Studies* 10 (1974): 1–28.

O'Kane, James. *Notes on the Rubrics of the Roman Ritual*. Dublin: James Duggey and Co., 1938.

Poling, James, and Donald Miller. *Foundations for Practical Theology*. Nashville: Abingdon Press, 1991.

Ramshaw, Elaine. *Ritual and Pastoral Care*. Philadelphia: Fortress Press, 1987.

Smolarski, Dennis. *How Not to Say Mass: A Guidebook for All Concerned about Authentic Worship*. Mahwah, New Jersey: Paulist, 1986.

Swayne, Sean. *Gather Around the Lord*. Dublin: The Columba Press, 1987.

Szafranski, Richard. "The One Who Presides At Eucharist." *Worship* 63, no. 4 (1989): 300-316.

Vincie, Catherine. "The Liturgical Assembly: Review and Reassessment." *Worship* 67, no. 2 (1993): 133.

———. "The Liturgical Assembly in Magisterial and Theological Literature and in the 1988 Rite of Christian Initiation of Adults." PhD diss., Catholic University of America, 1990.

Wallace, Ruth. *They Call Her Pastor: A New Role for Catholic Women*. Albany: State University of New York Press, 1992.

Walsh, Eugene. "Training the Muscles That Celebrate." *Liturgy* 17, no. 6 (1972): 6–9.

Weems, Lovett H. *Church Leadership: Vision, Team, Culture, and Integrity*. Nashville: Abingdon Press, 1993.

Works Cited

Whitehead, James D., and Evelyn Eaton Whitehead. *The Promise of Partnership: A Model for Collaborative Ministry.* San Francisco: Harper, 1993.

——. *Method in Ministry: Theological Reflection and Christian Ministry.* San Francisco: Harper, 1980.

Zualdi, Felix, CM. *The Sacred Ceremonies of the Low Mass.* New York: Benziger Brothers, 1911.